UNSTOPPABLE

UNSTOPPABLE

A MENTAL TRAINING GUIDE FOR FUELING PERFORMANCE

LANI SILVERSIDES

Mindful Performance, LLC

Published by Mindful Performance, LLC P.O. Box 670 York, ME 03909

Disclaimer: Every reasonable effort has been made to contact the copyright holders of materials in this book. If any have inadvertently been overlooked, the author would be glad to hear from them and make good in future editions any errors or omissions brought to their attention. The author is not engaged in rendering professional advice or services to the individual reader. This book is not intended to be a substitute for the medical advice of a licensed physician. The reader should consult with their doctor in any matters relating to his/her health. The author shall not be liable or responsible for any loss or damages allegedly arising from any information or suggestion in this book.

More resources and references available at www.lanisilversides.com

ACKNOWLEDGMENTS

I want to extend my sincere appreciation and gratitude to Dr. Amy Baltzell for being a wonderful teacher and mentor. She has served as an inspiration through her teaching and her books, particularly *Living in the Sweet Spot*. Her book and my first sport psychology class with Amy at Boston University got my journey started on helping others find the balance between high performance and well-being. There are many others who have had such an influence on me and this work. These include the many researchers who have done the hard work understanding and sharing the science behind the principles I use in this book. I mention their work throughout the text and in the *References and Resources*. Here is my (always) growing list of those to thank, in no particular order: Josh Summers, Angela Duckworth, Carol Dweck, Gabrielle Oettingen, Paul Gilbert, Jim Afremow, Martin Seligman, Kristin Neff, Christine Carter, Ryan Niemiec, Lea Waters, Kelly McGonigal, Neil Pasricha, BJ Fogg, Charles Duhigg, Jack Kornfield, Ellen Langer, Mihaly Csikszentmihalyi, Andy Cope, and Lucy Hone.

Beyond these amazing researchers and educators, I want to extend my gratitude to my #1 fan, my dad. Not only did he help me as editor, but he and my mom both have instilled in me a positive mindset, challenged me to get out of my comfort zone at all the right times, cheered me on through all the positive and challenging times, and serve as incredible role models.

Last but not least, my husband and two unstoppable girls inspire me in ways beyond what words can express. I hope what I can contribute to their lives is even a smidgen compared to what they've given me.

First things first!

Join the free online Resource Training Room. Activate your journal by registering it here to gain access:

UNSTOPPABLETRAININGJOURNAL.COM/ACTIVATE

NAME:

TABLE OF CONTENTS

FOREWORD   Becca Pizzi..9

INTRODUCTION...13

HUDDLE 1   LEADERSHIP
Learn how every person can and should practice their leadership skills.............................37

HUDDLE 2   STRENGTHS
Learn how to "be yourself" and use your strengths daily....................................55

HUDDLE 3   MINDSET
Learn about a growth mindset, how to think confidently, and why deliberate practice works 77

HUDDLE 4   VISION
Form your vision by first identifying your values. Then, set your goals................................103

HUDDLE 5   GRATITUDE
Learn how gratitude impacts your performance and well-being..133

HUDDLE 6   MINDFULNESS
Being fully engaged and in a flow state is known to be the state where peak performance happens.
Learn about mindfulness, attention, and flow..151

HUDDLE 7   COMPASSION
Learn the ultimate mental skill, and how it can help you bounce back from setbacks quickly. Also
learn how compassion for others is a difference maker..177

HUDDLE 8   RESILIENCE
Learn about the four core muscles for growing resilience......................................207

HUDDLE 9   THE SWEET SPOT
Learn how this all connects to being **unstoppable** and not only feeling good, but doing good 235

APPENDIX A   OFFSEASON REFLECTION 257

APPENDIX B   EXTRA WEEKLY CALENDARS...271

APPENDIX C   RECIPE SHEET FOR HABIT FORMATION......................................279

APPENDIX D   RECOVERY YOGA POSES REFERENCE SHEET................................280

APPENDIX E   COPING WITH INJURIES REFERENCE SHEET.............................282

APPENDIX F   IDENTIFYING CHARACTER STRENGTHS PAPER TEST......................284

REFERENCES AND RECOMMENDED READING..286

FOREWORD

BECCA PIZZI

FOREWORD

My dad inspired me to run when I was six years old when he took me to my first race. I have never stopped since. I love the opportunity to inspire others and to show the world you can do anything you put your mind to IF you believe in yourself. In 2016, I was the first American woman to complete the World Marathon Challenge. The World Marathon Challenge is seven marathons on seven continents in seven days. It all started with the first marathon in Novo, Antarctica. We then flew to and ran a marathon in Cape Town (Africa), Perth (Australia), Dubai (Asia), Lisbon (Europe), Cartagena (South America), and finally Miami (North America). I love to travel and love the ultimate test of endurance and strength. In 2018, I went back to defend my title and lower my world record. I will always cherish 2018, as my daughter Taylor met me at the finish and ran the last 100 yards with me, by my side, helping me make history.

Running marathons gives people a lot of time to be in their own head. We are having conversations with ourselves all the time, often battles. Being mentally strong is so important for success.

I rely on this strength, determination and hard work to carry me through both my training and races. I have come to realize how powerful the mind is and what you can do when you believe in yourself and have these mental skills.

When it comes down to competing, it is 90% mental. The physical part has been taken care of through hard work and training leading up to competition, but on race day, it's the mental part that gets me to the finish line.

I learned that in life you have to get really comfortable with being uncomfortable to survive. My biggest piece of advice is to find YOUR World Marathon Challenge, whatever it is YOU are passionate about. Believe in yourself, take chances, and dream big because when you do, anything is possible.

UNSTOPPABLE is the ultimate mental training guide and inspirational journal for any athlete. It really fuels my perspective in training (and many aspects of my life). I especially enjoy tracking the journey of my training for both running and life in general. The quotes and advice that Lani has in this beautiful high-quality journal are really valuable. I would definitely recommend to any runner – beginner to elite – for motivation and mental training and to track progress. Nice as a gift idea too for athletes or teams.

Take this book with you while you find YOUR World Marathon Challenge and we would love to hear how *UNSTOPPABLE* has changed your life the way it has changed ours!

Becca Pizzi
Endurance Runner
Two-Time World Marathon Champion
World Record Holder

INTRODUCTION

"YOU CANNOT GET THROUGH A SINGLE DAY WITHOUT HAVING AN IMPACT ON THE WORLD AROUND YOU. WHAT YOU DO MAKES A DIFFERENCE, AND YOU HAVE TO DECIDE WHAT KIND OF DIFFERENCE YOU WANT TO MAKE."

-JANE GOODALL

INTRODUCTION

There is more to being a champion athlete or team than just winning a championship at the end of the season. Being a champion is more than winning a tournament. It is a way to act. A way of *being* daily. Everyone can act like a champion. It is the way in which an athlete goes about the *process* that makes them a champion, not just the final outcome.

While society often defines victories in terms of wins and losses, developing the **character of a champion** such as expressing joy and kindness or developing resilience will equip you with skills that you can use in all facets of your life.

Winning, of course, is also fun and a worthy goal. Many studies have shown that developing the character of a champion helps you be the best performer you can be, regardless of wins and losses.

This journal is a 10-week guide that will help you develop your "mental muscles" and improve your mental toughness. It gives you tools to grow your leadership skills and build your own character strengths daily.

First, a bit on mental muscles.

While it is commonly acknowledged that lifting weights makes you physically stronger, there is a different kind of strength required to meet your fullest potential as a human being—mental strength. Research shows that this inner strength is something that can be improved. Your brain behaves like a muscle. It is what is in your brain that determines what you think, feel, say, and do. It is therefore undeniable that it is quite an important organ in your body. Therefore, you also need to train your brain! And, the fact is, you can train it just like you train your body.

Mental toughness is <u>not</u> about suppressing negative emotions or feelings and "gutting it out."

Mental toughness is <u>not</u> beating yourself up as a motivator to eliminate your mistakes or inadequacies in pursuit of your goals or in comparison to those around you.

Mental toughness is <u>not</u> doing whatever it takes (losing sleep, skipping breakfast, not listening to your body, not making time for your friends, etc.) in order to keep yourself afloat.

Rather, mental toughness is about resilience. It is having the courage to live by your own values. It is knowing where you are and where you want to go. For you. Not for other people or in comparison to others.

It is having a mindset that knows learning is limitless and allows failure and mistakes to serve as motivation instead of devastating setbacks.

It is knowing you have choices – how you view and react to each moment — and spending time or energy on what you can control and not on what you can't.

It is working toward experiencing more positive emotions such as gratitude, optimism, and joy, knowing that success revolves around happiness, not the other way around.

It is knowing that the path to joy and happiness often goes straight through stress, challenges, and adversity, not away from it.

It is developing passion and perseverance – a.k.a. grit!

Finally, mental toughness is about kindness and compassion – for yourself and for others.

Through building these mental muscles, you can and will improve your quality of performance in any domain (sport, school, job, etc.).

The leadership component of this journal is largely understanding that every athlete has not only the ability, but a responsibility, to be a leader.

The three leadership roles discussed (designated leader, peer leader, and self leader) are inspired by the National

Outdoor Leadership School (NOLS) curriculum. NOLS is a nonprofit global wilderness school that trains all of their students to boldly step forward to be leaders. Using the framework of wilderness expeditions, they have trained hundreds of thousands of students.

While a sports team or season may not involve a challenge of survival in the wilderness, there are some similarities between a team during their season and a NOLS expedition. The NOLS expeditions consist of a group of students together on a common journey. The students undoubtedly face obstacles and adversity along the way, and the group is almost always comprised of a variety of personalities, just like any sports team.

Through exploring the three leadership roles, you will be able to both find your comfort zone within them and possibly be challenged to go outside of that comfort zone and embrace new skills.

There is a sweet spot where your leadership roles and responsibilities, your mental muscles, and your own personality, strengths and style intersect. That intersection is the focus of this journal.

This is not where you are perfect. This is where you are unstoppable.

This is where you feel good and do good. This is the spot where you are contributing to your own life and to that of others around you.

Where you are UNSTOPPABLE!

THE SWEET SPOT
WHERE YOU ARE AT YOUR BEST. DOING GOOD FOR YOURSELF AND THOSE AROUND YOU.

MENTAL MUSCLES
KNOWING AND GROWING YOUR MENTAL MUSCLES. THE MORE YOU PRACTICE AND USE THEM, THE STRONGER THEY GET.

LEADERSHIP
LEADING THROUGH YOUR ACTIONS AND HOW THOSE ACTIONS INFLUENCE OTHERS.

STRENGTHS
KNOWING YOUR STRENGTHS AND BRINGING YOUR OWN PERSONALITY, STRENGTHS, AND STYLE FORWARD DAILY.

~BE YOU BRAVELY~

THE 3 LEADERSHIP ROLES

Every athlete has the opportunity to develop their leadership skills. The following leadership roles exist within a team. If you are an athlete or performer who isn't on a team, that doesn't leave you off the hook to work on your leadership roles. Read more about being a self and peer leader for all athletes and performers in Huddle 1.

DESIGNATED LEADER

+ Includes the captain(s).

+ Take the lead when the coach asks you to step up (such as to lead warmup).

+ Develop an action plan to accomplish a specific task (warm-up, clean up, etc.)

+ Resolve conflicts and be willing to seek additional help or support from adults.

+ Communicate effectively and openly with both coaches and teammates.

PEER LEADER

+ Proactively support the designated leader(s).

+ Seek clarity from designated leaders and coaches about game plans when needed.

+ Actively help move forward the goals and missions of the program.

+ Encourage teammates (and speak only positively about other teammates and coaches).

+ Pick up without being asked (for example, cleaning up the locker room or stands, water bottles, grabbing teammate's bags when the rain comes to get them under cover, etc.).

+ Treat everyone with respect.

+ Show teammates you believe in them.

+ Do good in your community and with your abilities. Give back.

SELF LEADER

+ Take responsibility for growing your own mental muscles.

+ Show up on time.

+ Bring proper gear to practice or competition.

+ Hydrate, eat, sleep, and take care of the needs of one's own human body and mind.

+ Get injuries or ailments taken care of.

+ Show gratitude to your supporters.

+ Do your share and stay organized.

+ Communicate with coaches.

"THE MOST POWERFUL LEADERSHIP TOOL IS YOUR OWN PERSONAL EXAMPLE."

-JOHN WOODEN

BE YOU BRAVELY

It takes courage to be yourself. This component of the sweet spot explores your own strengths and bringing those forward daily. More specifically, to become a champion of character, it will help you to look at *character* strengths. Research conducted all over the world shows that humans share the same 24 character strengths. Every individual possesses all 24 identified character strengths, just in different degrees. Huddle 2 will explore strengths so you **know them and grow them**!

> "THE THING THAT ALWAYS STRIKES ME IS HOW MUCH POWER ONE PERSON HAS. EVERYBODY HAS SO MUCH POWER TO HELP AND TO CHANGE IF THEY JUST EXERCISE IT AND GET AFTER IT."
> -PETE CARROLL

Each of the following are mental skills that act much like muscles. The more you practice them and use them, the stronger you get and the more they become part of you. This guide will focus on growing these six muscles. Each have their own huddle and week on which to focus.

MINDSET

+ Belief that learning is limitless and that failure and mistakes serve as motivation not as final or fatal setbacks.
+ Includes growth mindset, dealing with failure, confidence, self-talk, and deliberate practice.

MINDFULNESS & ATTENTION

+ Present moment nonjudgmental awareness. The ability to get into a flow state and experience optimal performance.
+ Includes mindfulness, attention, meditation, and flow.

VISION

+ The vehicle to drive you (your values) and where you want to go (your goals).
+ Includes values, goal setting, and WOOP mental strategy.

COMPASSION

+ Treating yourself and others with kindness.
+ Includes self-compassion, compassion, and kindness.

GRATITUDE

+ Learning to be more thankful and appreciative. Positive emotions about the present.
+ Includes gratitude and savoring.

RESILIENCE

+ Adapting in the face of adversity, stress, challenges, and/or setbacks.
+ Includes perspective, finding the awesome, hope/optimism, and humor.

COMING UP...

There are some basics to explore before getting into the Huddles (Chapters) and building your leadership, strengths, and mental muscles. In the last part of this introduction, you will find pages about the following:

✦**Your #1 Mental Skill** Your breath!

✦**The Science of Habit Formation** Throughout the journal and course you will be tasked to introduce new habits into your life that have the potential to improve performance and/or well-being. To get the most benefits from these skills, you need to do more than go through the motions of completing an exercise once. Reflect on what you have learned and see how it can fit into your life.

✦**Balancing Your Plate** Maximize the potential of your mind and body by considering the 7 essential elements that should be part of your every day (8 if you are a student as well!).

✦**Weekly Huddles** What to expect in the weekly huddles for the calendar and reflection pages.

"BREATHE,
BELIEVE, AND
BATTLE."

-KERRI WALSH JENNINGS

There is a skill that you all have inside you - your breath! Learning to use your breath properly can become your #1 mental skill. You may not always have your favorite socks, the best of weather, the good feelings pre-competition, or the crowd in your favor. But you ALWAYS have your breath with you.

WE TAKE ALMOST 1,000 BREATHS AN HOUR, 24 HOURS PER DAY

This gives you a lot of opportunities to improve your health, well-being, and awareness, and decrease stress and anxiety. Breathing affects every system in your body.

Breathing properly can reduce fatigue; decrease stress and muscle tension; calm your nerves; sharpen your focus; tune out distractions (including distracting or negative thoughts); and, help you sustain your efforts. **It can transform your health and your performance.** On the flip side, inefficient breathing can create sluggishness and tension.

One of the first things to occur when a person feels pressure is the acceleration of the heart rate. This can cause you to rush what you are doing (think of those moments where you rushed on a test or making a decision in a game). With a heightened heart rate, your mind will not be as clear or sharp. You have opportunities within practices and competitions where you can use your breath to help you reset yourself.

Practicing proper breathing can even contribute to better mechanics of movement (e.g. if a pitcher's breath occurs in their chest, it can cause tension in the shoulders and neck and therefore affect the mechanics of their pitch). The page that follows walks you through testing your breath and the six breathing techniques to practice. You will find video demonstrations guiding you through the practices in the online Resource Training Room.

First things first. You should test your breath to determine if you are breathing properly. Put one hand on your chest and one on your belly. Take a few deep breaths. Which hand is moving? The hand on your belly should be where the majority of the action occurs. This is known as "diaphragmatic breathing."

If you tend to keep your breath in your chest, it may take effort at the beginning to practice this new method. But with practice it will get easier and feel more natural.

To practice, it is best to start by lying down. Put a magazine or light book on your belly. Focus on breathing so that the book rises. When you get the hang of this, try sitting and standing, and test it again with your hand.

Learning to breathe in this way can help your performance and is a resource to reduce stress and/or tension. If you've seen a baby breathe, you'll see their belly rises. Re-train yourself to **breathe like a baby!**

INHALE

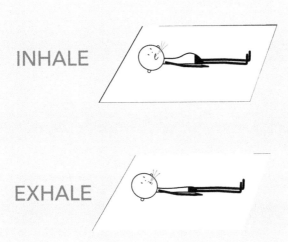

EXHALE

6 TECHNIQUES TO PRACTICE

Like everything in this guide, breathing properly and in a way that gives you all the benefits takes practice. Make sure you are enrolled in the online "course" that contains the Resource Training Room and watch the videos made for the six breathing techniques you can use to practice. Here is a list of the six techniques along with when they might be helpful. It will be beneficial to practice all six techniques and become familiar with how to use them in different situations. Eventually, you may find one that you particularly enjoy and you can then incorporate it into a daily habit.

#1 BREATH IN TIME
This technique is good for cultivating focus and control. It can also help you relax, calm down, and aid in quicker recovery.

#2 BREATH IN SPACE
This technique builds awareness.

#3 ALTERNATE NOSTRIL BREATHING
This technique cultivates balance throughout the body.

#4 COOLING BREATH
This technique is cooling and calming. It is good for the end of a workout.

#5 LION'S BREATH
This technique is energizing and warming.

#6 VICTORIOUS BREATH
This technique is warming. Using this technique through the yoga recovery workout (Appendix D and online) builds focus.

"WE ARE WHAT WE REPEATEDLY DO. EXCELLENCE, THEN, IS NOT AN ACT, BUT A HABIT."

-ARISTOTLE

Author Charles Duhigg in *The Power of Habit* identified the following 3 scientifically studied steps in habit formation:

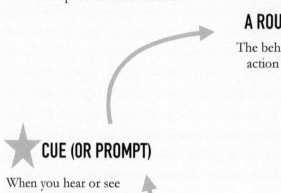

A ROUTINE

The behavior or action itself.

CUE (OR PROMPT)

When you hear or see something that makes you want to perform your habit. This could be a time of day, a location, actions of other people, pre-existing routines in your own life, or an emotional state.

THE REWARD

The benefit you gain from the action. This helps the brain determine if the loop is worth remembering in the future. If positive, it includes a spike of endorphins your brain gets from performing your routine.

Examples:

Cue—Waking up at 6:00 a.m.

Routine—Go for a run

Reward—Feel energized and happy for the day

Cue—Getting into bed at night

Routine—Think of three gratitudes from the day

Reward—Feel positive

You need the cue/prompt to get this habit loop started. You want to be aware of and build into your life triggers that develop good habits you want to keep and reduce the triggers for habits you want to get rid of. (For example, if you want to stop eating donuts, you need to not walk past the donut shop every morning by finding another route.) Notice in the diagram above the spike of endorphins happens at the reward step. If you want your habit to stick, you must repeat it. Over time, your brain will start to release the endorphins at the cue phase. **This is what helps you keep your habit!**

Dr. BJ Fogg out of Stanford University has developed a method he calls "Tiny Habits." Rather than starting big, such as asking yourself to meditate every day for 10 minutes, Tiny Habits® encourages you to set, you guessed it, *tiny* changes in your life. So small that you would feel silly NOT doing it. So small there is *no excuse* not to do it. For example, you might find or create a cue to meditate for two minutes each day and then add one or two additional minutes each week. After you decide the habit you want to add into your life (examples may include *writing one good thing about each day at night, meditating daily, positive self-talk, flossing,* or *stretching daily*), the steps to create your habit go like this:

STEP 1—IDENTIFY THE PROMPT.	This is something you already do in your day. It will become your cue. For example, flushing the toilet, stepping out of bed, putting your head on the pillow at the end of the day to sleep, washing your hands, tying your shoes, taking your shoes off, hanging the keys inside the door, etc.
STEP 2—WHAT'S THE ROUTINE?	What routine or habit are you adding into your life? Insert your Tiny Habit (the routine you've named) immediately following your prompt. For example, "After my feet hit the ground in the morning, I will take two deep breaths before moving on." (There is a mindfulness habit!)
STEP 3—CELEBRATE!	Reward yourself. Celebrate the fact you have performed your new habit. Examples of celebrations can include giving yourself a high-five, giving yourself a pat on the back, saying "YES!", giving yourself a couple of finger snaps, singing "We are the champions!", doing a little dance, etc.

In the Tiny Habits method, you create a "recipe," as BJ Fogg calls it, which is a plan that follows this template:

After _____[prompt]_____, I will _____[habit/routine]_____
and I will reward myself by _____[my celebration!]_____

You can go to *tinyhabits.com* to learn more. I encourage you to find ways to turn some of what you will learn in this book and course into habits. Feel free to start tiny! **Appendix C** has a recipe sheet you can use and reuse.

In order to optimize the power of your mind and your body, keep in mind the essential elements below:

Your goal is to balance your plate so each of these essential elements are part of your <u>every day</u>. They are the essentials to fuel your performance.

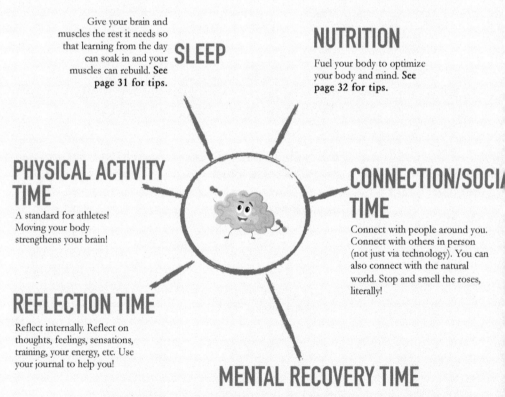

Give your brain and muscles the rest it needs so that learning from the day can soak in and your muscles can rebuild. **See page 31 for tips.**

SLEEP

NUTRITION

Fuel your body to optimize your body and mind. **See page 32 for tips.**

PHYSICAL ACTIVITY TIME

A standard for athletes! Moving your body strengthens your brain!

CONNECTION/SOCIAL TIME

Connect with people around you. Connect with others in person (not just via technology). You can also connect with the natural world. Stop and smell the roses, literally!

REFLECTION TIME

Reflect internally. Reflect on thoughts, feelings, sensations, training, your energy, etc. Use your journal to help you!

MENTAL RECOVERY TIME

This includes downtime and active recovery time in the form of "good goofing off". Good goofing off is a type of free-form attention that involves doing something you enjoy doing that doesn't require too much focus on the process. A kind of activity that engages the mind without simply being fed stimuli. Examples might include reading, baking, playing pickup with friends, playing frisbee on the lawn, daydreaming, doing a puzzle or another hobby.

The bottom line? **Spend time away from your sport, work, and technology. It helps your brain recharge.**

BE A CHAMPION SLEEPER REFERENCE SHEET

To be your best self on and off the field and in and out of the classroom, sleep is a must. Getting good sleep helps your brain learn and remember things, affects your growth, helps keep you from getting sick, and can improve your performance. Consider these 5 tips to become a champion sleeper from Jim Afremow's *The Champion's Mind*:

1 WHAT AMOUNT OF SLEEP HELPS YOU FEEL GOOD? THE KEY IS TO GET THE AMOUNT OF SLEEP THAT YOU NEED. RESEARCH SUGGESTS A MINIMUM OF 8 HOURS FOR MOST PEOPLE.

2 GIVE YOURSELF SOME DOWNTIME TO UNWIND BEFORE BED. JUST BEFORE BEDTIME IS NOT THE TIME TO SOLVE PROBLEMS. AVOID WATCHING TELEVISION OR SURFING THE INTERNET DURING THE HOUR BEFORE BEDTIME. IF YOU ARE KEYED UP, FIND THE MOST BORING BOOK OR ARTICLE YOU CAN AND READ A FEW PAGES TO GET SLEEPY.

3 TURN OFF OR DIM ANY OVERHEAD LIGHTS AS YOU NEAR BEDTIME. OTHERWISE, YOUR BRAIN WILL STILL THINK IT IS DAYTIME. USE A SLEE P MASK AND EARPLUGS IF NEEDED TO TUNE OUT NOISE AND LIGHT.

4 THINK ABOUT WHAT YOU WANT TO DREAM ABOUT, RATHER THAN DWELLING ON WHAT HAPPENED EARLIER TODAY OR WORRYING ABOUT WHAT IS ON TOMORROW'S AGENDA.

5 CHOOSE AN IDEA OR KEY WORD THAT WILL BE HELPFUL OR CALMING, AND THEN REPEAT IT OVER AND OVER AGAIN UNTIL YOU FALL ASLEEP.

NUTRITION REFERENCE SHEET

It is important you establish healthy eating and hydration habits.

Consider talking to your doctor and/or a nutritionist about your training and your body's needs. What is clear is that **food is fuel**. To get the most out of your body and mind, you need to fuel it well.

With healthy eating, you will:

FEEL BETTER.   RECOVER FASTER.

FEEL LESS FATIGUED.   MAINTAIN ENERGY.

FUEL YOUR PERFORMANCE.

IMPROVE SKIN AND BONE HEALTH.

PROMOTE YOUR OVERALL HEALTH.

Make sure you make a plan and are eating enough and well. This is an area that directly impacts your performance and is within your control. Every person is different. Reach out to your physician or a nutritionist to help.

DON'T FORGET TO HYDRATE!

GOALS WITH HYDRATION:

DELAY FATIGUE AND IMPROVE ABILITY TO REGULATE BODY HEAT. RECOVER QUICKER, SATISFY THIRST, AND REPLENISH WHAT IS LOST THROUGH SWEAT. BE WELL-HYDRATED *BEFORE* EXERCISE BEGINS NOT JUST DURING EXERCISE.

TIPS:

▷ YOU SHOULD CARRY A WATER BOTTLE (FULL OF WATER!) WITH YOU ALL DAY LONG.

▷ WHEN YOU ARE PROPERLY HYDRATED, YOUR PEE SHOULD BE CLEAR (NOT YELLOW!).

▷ WHEN YOU GET TIRED OF WATER, CONSIDER MAKING A HEALTHY SMOOTHIE.

YOUR TRAINING DAY ISN'T COMPLETED UNTIL YOU HAVE REFUELED!

There may be an 8th essential element. For <u>student</u>-athletes, balancing your plate will also include managing the demands of being a student as well as taking care of your mind and body. Being a champion in the classroom as well as being a champion of character should be **non-negotiable**. Consider these tips from Jim Afremow's *The Champion's Mind*:

1 SHOW UP TO *EVERY* CLASS AND BE ON TIME, WHETHER YOU FEEL LIKE IT OR NOT.

2 PAY CLOSE ATTENTION DURING CLASS BY TAKING GOOD NOTES.

3 PIPE UP—ASK QUESTIONS DURING CLASS, FORM STUDY GROUPS, AND MEET WITH YOUR TEACHERS AS NEEDED.

4 STUDY A LITTLE BIT *EACH DAY* RATHER THAN CRAMMING AT THE END. TRAIN YOUR BRAIN TO BE READY TO WORK AT CERTAIN, CONSISTENT TIMES.

5 EARN GOOD GRADES BY WORKING HARD AND SMART— THERE ARE NO SHORTCUTS OR MAGIC TRICKS FOR SUCCESS. DON'T CUT CORNERS ON YOUR EDUCATION.

6 BELIEVE THAT YOU CAN EXCEL IN ANY SUBJECT IF YOU PUT YOUR MIND TO IT.

From this point on, each huddle includes a topic for you to practice and/or a muscles to grow! To be your best self, weekly training includes both the physical and the mental training. Each week, at the end of the huddle, are calendar and reflection pages. Here, there is a space for you to:

1. Set your intention for the week.

This exercise is to choose ONE WORD that you will keep in mind for the week. You may repeat words as well. Perhaps you have a word for your entire season or year. Examples of one word intentions might be:

focus, fun, smile, laugh, compete, joy, savor, grateful, confidence, family, integrity, commitment, authentic, lead, perspective, celebrate, trust, hope, engage, love, strength

2. Keep a daily log. This may include the following:

▶ Mileage (for runners, especially) or workout plan.

▶ Important milestones.

▶ Appointments/Practice times/Competitions

3. Write your daily SPEC! (Small Positive Enjoyable or Cool thing from each day).

Our brains natural negativity bias makes it hard sometimes to find the good. It's not your fault! It's the way our brain works. But you can train your brain to find the good. Start training your brain daily by writing even just one thing that went well from your day.

4. Reflect. Reflect on both your strengths and challenges you are facing.

LETTER TO YOUR FUTURE SELF

Here you are at the start of your season. Write a letter to yourself to read at the end of the season. Give your future you a pep talk. Consider highlighting now what matters most to you as you look forward to your season.

CHALK TALK SPOT

THROUGHOUT THE JOURNAL YOU WILL SEE THESE CHALK TALK SPOTS. THEY WILL GIVE YOU REMINDERS OR SIMPLE TIPS

HUDDLE 1

LEADERSHIP

"A LEADER IS ONE WHO KNOWS THE WAY, GOES THE WAY, AND SHOWS THE WAY."

-JOHN MAXWELL

HUDDLE 1
LEADERSHIP

IN THIS HUDDLE:

▷ What are the leadership roles that I can take on individually and/or within a team?

▷ What are the leadership responsibilities I am committed to?

▷ What do I have control over with respect to my performance and in competition?

Anyone can be a leader. Leadership is not necessarily a position or a title. It is taking responsibility for your own actions and for your role as a teammate or in your community.

In fact, as a member of a team or an athlete in your community, you have both an opportunity and a responsibility to develop your leadership. On a team, you may be asked to step into different roles in different situations. On a day that the captain is not at practice, your coach may call on you to be the "designated leader" for the day. This is your opportunity to step up into that responsibility. But even if you are not formally designated as a team leader, you can always assume the roles of self leadership and peer leadership.

EACH AND EVERY ATHLETE IS A LEADER THROUGH THEIR ACTIONS AND HOW THOSE ACTIONS INFLUENCE OTHERS.

"The culture precedes positive results. It doesn't get tacked on as an afterthought on your way to the victory stand. Champions behave like champions before they're champions; they have a winning standard of performance before they are winners."

–Bill Walsh

SELF
LEADER

You can start growing your self leadership skills by developing your character (including using your strengths and building your mental muscles). How does building your mental muscles connect with leadership?

Emotions and your attitude are contagious. So is your smile and your positivity. Doing kind things for others makes them more likely to do kind things for others. That means that being a leader in your school, community, on your team, or at your job can actually be about you doing small things for yourself and those around you to improve your well-being and attitude and make a positive impact on others. People around you are just as likely to catch your happiness and positivity as they are your cold or flu. Which would you rather share with others?

EXAMPLE RESPONSIBILITIES OF A SELF LEADER

- [ ] Take responsibility for growing your own mental muscles and character strengths (Huddles 2-8).
- [ ] Bring proper gear to practice and competition.
- [ ] Hydrate, eat, sleep, and take care of the needs of your own body and mind.
- [ ] Get injuries or ailments taken care of.
- [ ] Show gratitude to your supporters.
- [ ] Do your share and stay organized.
- [ ] Show up on time.
- [ ] Communicate with coaches.
- [ ] Keep your body language positive.

PEER
LEADER

Build upon your self leadership to become a peer leader. For individual athletes, focusing on building your peer leadership skills involves thinking of your actions and contributions and how they impact those around you. This list includes example responsibilities of a peer leader. The next page includes a list of *additional* responsibilities for those on a team.

EXAMPLE RESPONSIBILITIES OF A PEER LEADER

☐ Treat everyone with respect (including opponents, officials, etc.).

☐ Do good in your community and with your abilities. Give back.

☐ Make others feel valued.

☐ Be the example for others to follow.

☐ Lead with character.

☐ Showcase your mental muscles (knowing and growing them happens in self-leadership).

☐ Act (and be!) positive.

☐ Focus on the process versus the outcome.

☐ Let go of judgements.

PEER
LEADER

Within a team setting you can practice peer leadership in multiple ways throughout a season or year. For example, peer leaders avoid gossip and criticizing teammates behind their backs. They are enthusiastic followers of designated leaders, coaches, and the mission of the team, seeking clarity when needed and supporting teammates without needing to be asked to do so. Consider the list on the previous page as well as the list below to develop your peer leadership skills.

ADDITIONAL RESPONSIBILITIES OF A PEER LEADER WITHIN A TEAM SETTING

☐ Proactively support the designated leader(s).

☐ Seek clarity from designated leaders and coaches about game plans when needed.

☐ Actively help move forward the goals and missions of the program.

☐ Encourage teammates (and speak only positively about other teammates and coaches).

☐ Pick up without being asked (for example, cleaning up the locker room, stands, water bottles, grabbing teammates' bags when the rain comes to get them under cover, etc.).

☐ Show teammates you believe in them.

DESIGNATED
LEADER

A designated leader is an appointed member of a team. She or he can delegate and should collaborate whenever possible. However, the designated leader cannot turn their back on responsibility or accountability. They don't blame others and instead create solutions and involve everyone. Designated leaders, especially on a big team, should make an effort to get to know every individual on their team. The designated leaders of a team are also often the ones who communicate with the coaches. They are on the "ground floor" and know the ins and outs of the team and needs of individuals. These leaders must be trustworthy and honest and willing to speak openly with coaches.

EXAMPLE RESPONSIBILITIES OF A DESIGNATED LEADER

- [ ] Showcase their self and peer leadership skills.
- [ ] Includes the captain(s) if you have them.
- [ ] Take the lead when the coach asks you to step up (such as to lead warmup).
- [ ] Develop an action plan to accomplish a specific task (warm-up, clean up, etc.)
- [ ] Resolve conflicts and be willing to seek additional help or support from adults.
- [ ] Communicate effectively and openly with both coaches and teammates.

MY
LEADERSHIP

Name 3 leaders you admire most. For each, write 3 qualities you admire about them:

LEADER:	3 QUALITIES I ADMIRE ABOUT THE LEADER:

It takes one to know one! Take a look at those qualities you wrote and know that you have them in yourself. You cannot see them without having them in yourself as well.

Write the qualities below that you see as strengths of yours:

Write which qualities you would like to cultivate more often:

Given the following qualities and responsibilities noted of self and peer leaders, write an example of how you can *practice* and demonstrate these skills.

LEADERSHIP SKILL/ RESPONSIBILITY	WAY TO PRACTICE AND DEMONSTRATE SKILL
Treat everyone with respect	
Give back to your community	
Lead with character	
Make others feel valued	
Take care of own mind and body (sleep, etc.)	
Show gratitude	
Encourage others	
Be (and act!) positive	
Keep your body language positive	

Fill in the blank spaces above with other responsibilities you are committed to or came up with in the previous exercise and/or your team has deemed important.

Talent is not necessary for MANY aspects of being an athlete. Here are some things that don't require talent. These are all within your control. Bring these skills with you daily. A key element of good leadership is focusing on what you can control and letting go of what you can't.

YOUR EFFORT.

CHEERING & SUPPORTING TEAMMATES.

YOUR ATTITUDE.

SHOWING UP PREPARED.

BEING COACHABLE.

"I PUSH MYSELF TO BE THE BEST I CAN BE. I DON'T WORRY ABOUT WHAT OTHER PEOPLE ARE DOING, AND I DON'T THINK ABOUT THINGS I CAN'T CONTROL."

-ANNIKA SORENSTAM

Make a list of the components of your performance that you can control:

Make a list of the components of your performance that you can NOT control:

CHALK
TALK SPOT
BUTTERFLIES ARE A-OKAY!
THEY ARE YOUR BODY'S WAY
TO PREPARE YOU FOR A
CHALLENGE. MORE ON
PG. 211

LEADER (FAMOUS OR OTHERWISE) I LOOK UP TO AND WOULD LIKE TO EMULATE:...........................

....

DATE   WORKOUT/PLAN/FOCUS

MON

TODAY'S **SPEC**:

TUES

TODAY'S **SPEC**:

WED

TODAY'S **SPEC**:

Reminder: Your daily **SPEC** is a small positive, enjoyable, and/or cool thing from your day!

WORKOUT/PLAN/FOCUS

DATE

THU

TODAY'S **SPEC**:

FRI

TODAY'S **SPEC**:

SAT

TODAY'S **SPEC**:

SUN

TODAY'S **SPEC**:

"LIFE'S MOST PERSISTENT AND URGENT QUESTION IS, 'WHAT ARE YOU DOING FOR OTHERS?'"

–MARTIN LUTHER KING, JR.

TIME FOR T.W.C.

What is this week's challenge or something that did not go well? If it is something you can control and improve upon, make a plan for the coming week. If it is not something you can control, then consider writing it here and then turning the page as a symbolic gesture of letting it go.

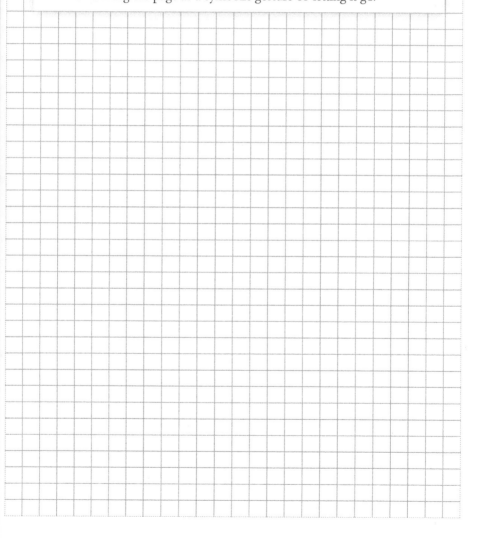

CHECK IN... HOW ARE YOU DOING BALANCING YOUR PLATE <u>DAILY</u>?

Refer to page 30 if you need a refresher

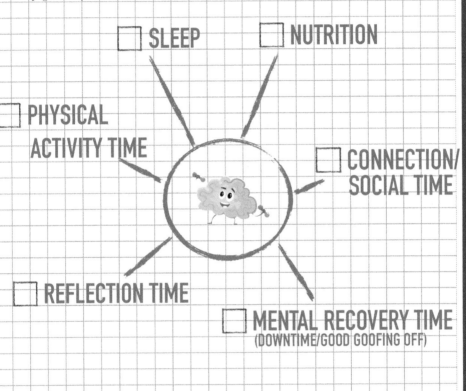

- ☐ SLEEP
- ☐ NUTRITION
- ☐ PHYSICAL ACTIVITY TIME
- ☐ CONNECTION/ SOCIAL TIME
- ☐ REFLECTION TIME
- ☐ MENTAL RECOVERY TIME (DOWNTIME/GOOD GOOFING OFF)

What steps will you take to make sure each of these essential elements are part of your upcoming week?

HUDDLE 2

STRENGTHS

"TRUE POWER COMES FROM WITHIN. WHAT WE SEEK, WE ALREADY HAVE."

-THICH NHAT HAHN

HUDDLE 2
STRENGTHS

IN THIS HUDDLE:
▷ What are character strengths and what is the research behind them?

▷ What are my signature strengths?

▷ What are new ways I can contribute daily to my team using my strengths?

Character strengths have been shown to be the foundation for thriving. As mentioned in this guide's introduction, every person can become a champion of character. Character is a collection of positive characteristics shown through thoughts, feelings, and actions. Professors Martin Seligman and Christopher Peterson conducted research around the world and identified 24 character strengths that are shared, regardless of race, class, gender, location, etc. Every individual possesses all 24 identified character strengths, just in different degrees. They are organized under 6 virtue categories. On the VIA Institute website, you can take a free survey and learn more about your specific 24 character strengths. If you don't have access to a computer, you can go to **Appendix F** to take a short version paper test.

Steps for you to discover your strengths:

1. Go to viacharacter.org

2. Register to take the free survey. You'll choose the VIA Youth Survey for ages 10-17 or the VIA Adult for ages 18 and up.

3. Answer the questions. This will take approximately 10 minutes.

4. When prompted at the end, enter the research code: UNSTOPPABLE

5. Download your free report and look at your results with an eye toward identifying your top strengths, also known as your *signature strengths*.

Research shows using your strengths can help you be happier, strengthen your relationships, manage problems, boost confidence, reduce stress, and accomplish goals. These are all areas where each member of a team can help themselves and contribute to the greater good of their team.

Studies show focusing on using your signature strengths (approximately your top five) improves your overall well-being. Throughout this book you will be asked to reflect back on what strengths you have used or have spotted in others.

Bringing your signature character strengths into that sweet spot is an example of a way for you to focus on **being you bravely.** Rather than going to the bottom of your list for what you possess (but maybe doesn't come as easily), you can instead focus on the top strengths you already exhibit! In fact, research indicates that you grow your strengths by using them often and in new ways whenever possible. Athletes (and people in general) are often quite good at looking at the negative and what needs to improve. This section (and each week that follows) will challenge you to spot and use your strengths, both character strengths and those skills or athletic strengths specific to your sport or performance realm.

How do you know what are really your strengths? Strengths are:

1. **Things you do well.**

2. **Things you do often.**

3. **Things that give you energy.**

THE VIA
CLASSIFICATION OF STRENGTHS

Each of the 24 strengths falls under a category among 6 virtues.

WISDOM & KNOWLEDGE

CREATIVITY: Originality; adaptive; ingenuity
CURIOSITY: Interest; novelty-seeking;
exploration; openness to experience
JUDGMENT: Critical thinking; thinking
things through; open-minded
LOVE OF LEARNING: Mastering new skills
& topics; systematically adding to knowledge
PERSPECTIVE: Wisdom; providing wise
counsel; taking the big picture view

COURAGE

BRAVERY: Valor; not shrinking from fear;
speaking up for what's right
PERSEVERANCE: Persistence; industry;
finishing what one starts
HONESTY: Authenticity; integrity
ZEST: Vitality; enthusiasm; vigor; energy;
feeling alive and activated

JUSTICE

TEAMWORK: Citizenship; social
responsibility; loyalty
FAIRNESS: Just; not letting feelings bias
decisions about others
LEADERSHIP: Organizing group activities;
encouraging a group to get things done

HUMANITY

LOVE: Both loving and being loved; valuing
close relations with others
KINDNESS: Generosity; nurturance; care;
compassion; altruism; "niceness"
SOCIAL INTELLIGENCE: Emotional
intelligence; aware of motives/feelings of self/
others, knowing what makes other people tick

TEMPERANCE

FORGIVENESS: Mercy; accepting others'
shortcomings; giving people a second chance
HUMILITY: Modesty; letting one's
accomplishments speak for themselves
PRUDENCE: Careful; cautious; not taking
undue risks
SELF-REGULATION: Self-control;
disciplined; managing impulses & emotions

TRANSCENDENCE

APPRECIATION OF BEAUTY &
EXCELLENCE: Awe; wonder; elevation
GRATITUDE: Thankful for the good;
expressing thanks; feeling blessed
HOPE: Optimism, future-mindedness; future
orientation
HUMOR: Playfulness; bringing smiles to
others; lighthearted
SPIRITUALITY: Religiousness; faith, purpose;
meaning

"DON'T LET WHAT
YOU CAN'T DO
INTERFERE WITH
WHAT YOU CAN DO."

–JOHN WOODEN

FIND YOUR
STRENGTHS

MY SIGNATURE STRENGTHS

If you used the survey to help you identify your top strengths, consider looking at the top seven and choosing the three to six that most resonate with you. Those are your signature strengths. They are the ones you do well, do often, and that give you energy.

Put your signature strengths here:

Pick ONE of your top strengths and imagine your life without using or having it. What would that be like?

61

"MAKE THE MOST
OF YOURSELF, FOR
THAT IS ALL THERE
IS OF YOU."

-RALPH WALDO EMERSON

USE YOUR
STRENGTHS

For each of your signature strengths, write out ways in which you can use them in your sport or performance domain. Ideas are given on the next page for each of the 24 strengths.

STRENGTH:	WAYS TO USE MY STRENGTHS IN MY SPORT/PERFORMANCE REALM:

EXAMPLE WAYS TO USE EACH STRENGTH

CREATIVITY: Offer a creative solution to a problem that your teammate or team faces (their problem could be in or outside of your sport).

CURIOSITY: Find something new about your practice field or environment that you've never noticed before.

JUDGMENT (CRITICAL THINKING): Ask one or two clarifying questions of a teammate who approaches game day preparation differently than you.

LOVE OF LEARNING: Learn and practice a new skill or move.

PERSPECTIVE: Help counsel a teammate who is disappointed about their playing time or performance.

BRAVERY: Speak up in the locker room when teammates are talking about something or someone inappropriately.

PERSEVERANCE: Fight through a tough workout even when you want to stop.

HONESTY: Bring your authentic self to practice and share with your captain(s), coach(es), and/or teammates a "fun fact" about you people might not know.

ZEST: Bring a lot of energy to cheer for your teammates during practice/competition.

TEAMWORK: Savor a positive team event or game/competition from the past and share it with the team.

FAIRNESS: Seek out someone on your team who has been left out in the past and go out of your way to include them.

LEADERSHIP: Organize a team dinner or event to do together.

LOVE: Surprise a teammate (or all) with a handmade gift or card prior to the next competition.

KINDNESS: Help the staff members clean up the field, court, or gym space after a game.

SOCIAL INTELLIGENCE: Start up a conversation that has to do with something outside your sport with a teammate whom you perhaps do not normally talk to about that stuff.

FORGIVENESS: Forgive yourself for making a mistake while performing.

HUMILITY: Ask your coach to give you feedback on skills/areas for growth.

PRUDENCE: Make a list of your commitments this week in and outside of your sport and think through if they are all necessary. Should you make any adjustments or decisions that will improve your chances of getting adequate sleep, rest, and relaxation?

SELF-REGULATION: The next time you feel frustrated in practice or competition, notice it, and then take a few deep breaths and move on to the next action or play.

APPRECIATION OF BEAUTY & EXCELLENCE: Spend a few minutes at your field, court, or competition space without distractions so you can take it all in and appreciate it. Or, go watch professional athletes in your sport and appreciate their skill.

GRATITUDE: Offer during warmups that you and each person on your team say something they are grateful for from the day.

HOPE: After a loss in competition, speak positively to your team about the future and capabilities of the team.

HUMOR: In an appropriate moment during practice (or after), tell a joke to your team.

SPIRITUALITY: Take in the present moment during your next team gathering. Allow yourself the opportunity to find meaning in what you and your team seek to do during the season.

LESSER
STRENGTHS

LESSER STRENGTHS

Athletes are accustomed to working on their weaknesses, especially when it comes to skills and improvement within their performance domain. When it comes to *character* strengths, the ones that may show up on the bottom of the list are just strengths that don't come as easily. While focusing on your signature strengths has a ton of benefits, it doesn't mean you need not ever work on your lesser strengths as well. What are some strengths that fell to the bottom of your list *that you want to strengthen and grow* that will help you in performance?

Lesser strengths:	Ways I can work on them:

PERFORMANCE
STRENGTHS

Being on a team provides a pathway to develop character in positive ways, whether that team is through athletics, performing arts, music, or even within a job. Knowing, using, and spotting character strengths in oneself and others is a direct way to increase well-being and build character. Within athletics and performance, knowing and using your strengths as a performer is critical for success. If *too* much time is spent focused on your weakness or where you fall short, you may miss opportunities to showcase your strengths and find the best role for you within a team.

Top 10 things I respect about myself as a performer:

1.

2.

3.

4.

5.

6.

7.

8.

9.

10.

Write your own scouting report here. Make sure you are explicit about your strengths as as performer. Most scouting reports also include lesser strengths for an individual performer or areas where improvement is needed. For those areas, you may consider coming back here when setting goals in Huddle 4.

YOUR WORTH IS NOT DEFINED BY YOUR PERFORMANCE.

One more note before moving on: "Compete" comes from the Latin origin meaning "strive together." This means it depends on other people, too. Sometimes in our society people turn "compete" inward and focus on themselves and how they compare to others around them. Instead, I urge you to "strive together," support others, and lift everyone up in all that you do.

THOUGH WE LIVE IN AN ACHIEVEMENT-ORIENTED AND COMPETITIVE SOCIETY, EACH EVENT THAT HAS A POSSIBLE OUTCOME IS <u>NOT</u> AN OPPORTUNITY TO DEFINE YOU AS A HUMAN BEING OR YOUR SELF-WORTH. THE VALUE OF <u>YOU</u> CANNOT BE MEASURED BY AN OUTCOME, A PERFORMANCE, OR A SCORE.

MAKE IT ABOUT THE PROCESS.

NOT THE OUTCOME.

The sweet spot is a place where the process matters more than the outcome. Here are reasons to focus on the process:

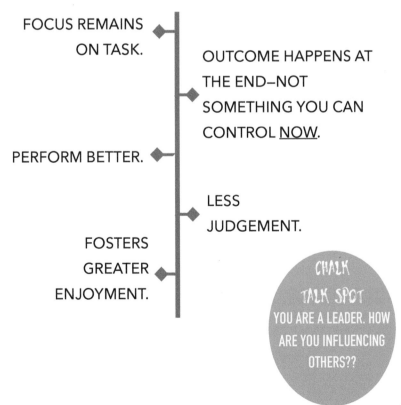

FOCUS REMAINS ON TASK.

OUTCOME HAPPENS AT THE END–NOT SOMETHING YOU CAN CONTROL <u>NOW</u>.

PERFORM BETTER.

LESS JUDGEMENT.

FOSTERS GREATER ENJOYMENT.

CHALK TALK SPOT
YOU ARE A LEADER. HOW ARE YOU INFLUENCING OTHERS??

THIS WEEK'S INTENTION IN ONE WORD:

....

STRENGTH I LOVE THE MOST ABOUT MYSELF: ....

....

DATE	WORKOUT/PLAN/FOCUS

MON

TODAY'S **SPEC**:

TUES

TODAY'S **SPEC**:

WED

TODAY'S **SPEC**:

Remember BJ Fogg's Tiny Habits® recipe (page 29)? If you are having a hard time remembering to write your SPEC for each day, now would be a good time to make a plan for inserting it as a habit. This practice is so good for your brain and training it to find the good, it is important to find a place for it daily!:

After _____, I will _____ and I will reward myself by _____

[prompt]   [write my SPEC   [my celebration!]
small positive enjoyable or cool thing
from my day – What went well?]

DATE | WORKOUT/PLAN/FOCUS | DATE

THU

TODAY'S **SPEC**:

FRI

TODAY'S **SPEC**:

SAT

TODAY'S **SPEC**:

SUN

TODAY'S **SPEC**:

"ALWAYS REMEMBER THAT YOU ARE ABSOLUTELY
UNIQUE. JUST LIKE EVERYONE ELSE."
-MARGARET MEAD

ZOOMING IN

Creativity	Curiousity	Judgement	Perspective	Bravery	Perseverance

Zest	Honesty	Social Intelligence	Kindness	Love	Leadership

WHAT WENT WELL this week in performance (or practice/training, if applicable)?

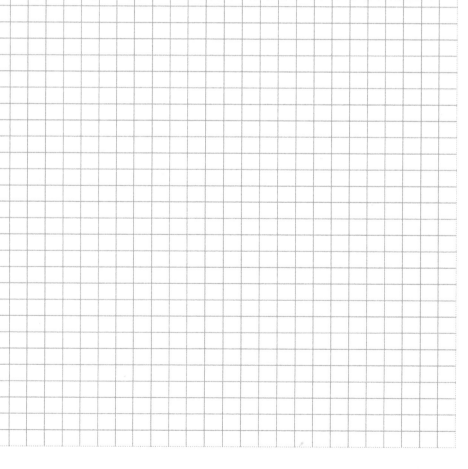

72

ON YOUR STRENGTHS...

Fairness	Teamwork	Forgiveness	Love of Learning	Gratitude	Spirituality

Self-Regulation	Humility	Appreciation of Beauty	Prudence	Hope	Humor

After reflecting on what went well, circle at least **three strengths you used** this week in practice, competition, or otherwise and give examples of each. Consider also your **signature strengths** and make sure you are practicing using those daily!

My signature strengths:

☑
☑
☑
☑
☑

TIME FOR T.W.C.

What is this week's challenge or something that did not go well? If it is something you can control and improve upon, make a plan for the coming week. If it is not something you can control, then consider writing it here and then turning the page as a symbolic gesture of letting it go.

THINK YOU NEED TO PULL AN ALL-NIGHTER? THINK AGAIN!

STAYING UP 24 HOURS GIVES YOU THE SAME REACTION TIME AS .1 ALCOHOL IN YOUR SYSTEM. THAT'S OVER THE LEGAL LIMIT. YOUR REACTION TIME IS SO BAD IT'S DANGEROUS. IN SOME STATES, IT'S ILLEGAL TO DRIVE AFTER STAYING AWAKE FOR 24 HRS AND IS PUNISHABLE IN THE SAME CLASS AS INTOXICATED DRIVING. SLEEPINESS IMPAIRS YOUR PERFORMANCE. PRIORITIZE SLEEP!

CHECK IN...HOW ARE YOU DOING BALANCING YOUR PLATE DAILY?

Refer to page 30 if you need a refresher

☐ SLEEP   ☐ NUTRITION

☐ PHYSICAL ACTIVITY TIME

☐ CONNECTION/ SOCIAL TIME

☐ REFLECTION TIME

☐ MENTAL RECOVERY TIME
(DOWNTIME/GOOD GOOFING OFF)

What steps will you take to make sure each of these essential elements are part of your upcoming week?

HUDDLE 3

MINDSET

"ATTITUDE IS A CHOICE. WHAT YOU THINK YOU CAN DO, WHETHER POSITIVE OR NEGATIVE, CONFIDENT OR SCARED, WILL MOST LIKELY HAPPEN."

-PAT SUMMITT

HUDDLE 3
MINDSET

IN THIS HUDDLE:

▷ What mindset is best for learning and growing as an athlete to become the best I can be?

▷ What is deliberate practice and how does that help?

▷ What do I do when I make a mistake?

▷ How do I grow my confidence?

▷ What is my go-to self-talk performance statement?

Your mindset muscle is a way of describing your underlying beliefs and set of attitudes toward your life, learning, and events. Psychologist and author Carol Dweck is the pioneer of research on this topic and coined the terms "growth mindset" and "fixed mindset." In a **growth mindset**, people believe that their most basic abilities can be developed through dedication and hard work—brains and talent are just the starting point. This view creates a love of learning and a resilience that is essential for great accomplishment. Virtually all people who have achieved greatness have had these qualities.

In a **fixed mindset**, people believe their basic qualities, like their intelligence or talent, are simply fixed traits. They spend their time documenting their intelligence or talent instead of developing them. They also believe that inborn talent is far more important than effort in creating success.

Research has shown repeatedly that the growth mindset strongly enhances motivation and achievement and that you can learn to change from a fixed mindset to a growth mindset. As an athlete, student, and/or performer, a growth mindset leads you to embrace learning, to welcome challenges, mistakes, and feedback, and to understand the role of effort in developing talent.

This goes beyond just "thinking" your mindset matters. Scientific research has uncovered physical changes to people's brains following repeated practice and effort.

79

"WHETHER YOU
THINK YOU CAN OR
YOU THINK YOU
CAN'T, YOU'RE
RIGHT."

–HENRY FORD

THE FIXED MINDSET	SITUATION OR EVENT	THE GROWTH MINDSET
"I am not as good."	Lost the race	"I pushed too hard in the first lap."
"I am better than everyone else."	Won the race	"My focus on my rhythm helped me through the last lap."
"You were the best out there!"	Post game comments from parents, teachers, & other supporters	"You worked so hard out there. I loved watching you play."
"This is too hard."	Facing obstacles	"This is going to take some extra time and effort."
"I really messed up."	Mistakes	"This is an opportunity for me to grow."
"The referee was terrible today. She/he was the reason we lost."	Setbacks	"We could have put in more effort today and worked better as a team."
"That was a perfect shot."	Basketball coach	"I see that you held your follow through on that shot."

Think of your brain like it's a muscle. It can get stronger (smarter!) the more you exercise it through **effort, trying new things**, and **learning from mistakes**. The more compassionate you can be toward yourself when you make a mistake, the better you feel (more on this in Huddle 7) and the more likely you are to recover quickly and still try new things.

Brain plasticity is the scientific term for the ability for your brain to grow and change. Practice and repetition actually create new neural pathways. This is hugely important for an athlete who wants to develop new skills.

PRACTICE DOES NOT MAKE "PERFECT". PRACTICE MAKES PROGRESS.

For both physical and mental skills, practice helps you develop new mental representations in your brain that will be used later to execute the skill you are developing! Of course, practicing the right way is important so you don't develop these mental representations for a "bad" habit.

DELIBERATE
PRACTICE

"Just keep practicing and you will improve" is not *entirely* true. It takes a certain kind of practice — what Swedish psychologist Anders Ericsson calls **deliberate practice**. With the deliberate practice mindset, the idea is that anyone can improve, but only with the correct approach. To make this most useful to you, it is first helpful to understand the science behind deliberate practice. In her book *Grit*, Angela Duckworth outlines this as the following:

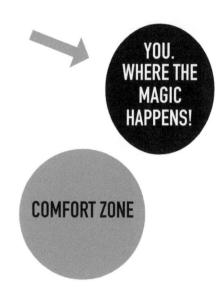

YOU. WHERE THE MAGIC HAPPENS!

COMFORT ZONE

Deliberate practice requires:

▸ **A clearly defined stretch goal**

▸ **Full concentration and effort**

▸ **Immediate and informative feedback**

▸ **Repetition with reflection and refinement** (p. 137)

Deliberate practice is purposeful, and it includes a teacher or coach. Deliberate practice takes you out of your comfort zone and stretches your abilities. You practice something you can't YET do, and then focus on finding a way if and when you fall short.

It's not always *try again*. Sometimes it's *try differently*. A coach or teacher is there to give you feedback along the way. Once you spend time with deliberate practice, it can be helpful to change the way you view and experience it. In *Grit*, Duckworth quotes Terry Laughlin, a swim coach, who says, "Deliberate practice can feel wonderful...It's all about in-the-moment **self-awareness without judgment**. It's about relieving yourself of the judgment that gets in the way of **enjoying the challenge**." (p. 140)

So, next time after some hard, purposeful, deliberate practice stretching your abilities and pulling you out of your comfort zone, you can say,

"PRACTICE WAS HARD TODAY AND IT WAS AWESOME!"

The San Antonio Spurs, coached and led currently by Gregg Popovich, are known to have the team mantra "Pound the rock" used from Jacob Riis's stonecutter analogy:

> "WHEN NOTHING SEEMS TO HELP, I GO AND LOOK AT A STONECUTTER HAMMERING AWAY AT HIS ROCK PERHAPS A HUNDRED TIMES WITHOUT AS MUCH AS A CRACK SHOWING IN IT. YET AT THE HUNDRED AND FIRST BLOW IT WILL SPLIT IN TWO, AND I KNOW IT WAS NOT THAT BLOW THAT DID IT, BUT ALL THAT HAD GONE BEFORE."
> –JACOB RIIS

Though a stone may show no signs of cracking, you never know which blow will make it finally break. While you may be used to or seek instant gratification, this long-term view on what you do may help you grow your "grit muscle" among other things. Deliberate practice is hard. Persevering through challenges and setbacks is hard. When you have passion and purpose for something you are working toward, keep pounding the rock!

SELF-AWARENESS
WITHOUT JUDGEMENT

What are the skills you want to practice and improve on, with the help of your coach, that are a bit outside of your comfort zone?

VISUALIZE

What about when you can't practice? Perhaps you have an injury or need to give your body some physical rest. Imagery to the rescue! Imagery is another tool many performers use, not just in the face of injuries but to prepare them for meeting their goals. Have you ever rehearsed what you are going to say before a presentation or before speaking to a friend about something serious? That's imagery! Have you ever produced saliva in your mouth even BEFORE eating something sour such as Sour Patch Kids? Perhaps you open the bag and grab a handful and your mouth starts to water. That's imagery! Your brain imagined the sour taste and produced the saliva before to happened. If I told you to imagine nails on a chalkboard, and you REALLY imagined hearing long nails screeching across a chalk board, you might get grossed out or shiver. That's imagery!

Our brain doesn't know the difference between what is actually happening and what you are imagining. This makes it a powerful tool to practice. You can prepare yourself for an event so that when you get there it feels like you've been there before, even if you haven't. Michael Phelps is known as one of the best visualizers. When his goggles fogged up and he couldn't see underwater in the 2009 Olympics in Beijing, it didn't matter. Because he had already visualized the race and every stroke and move he needed to make, he still won the race (and seven others at that Olympics!).

What it takes to do it well and right (and deliberately!):

1. **Think of it like playing a movie in your head.**

2. **Think about the sights, sounds, smells, temperature, and any other senses or environmental conditions (raining, windy, etc.).**

3. **Get your emotions into it. How do you feel (in the performance)? When you get really good at this practice, you will even find your heart rate rise like it might during the event.**

4. **Choose a perspective. You can view the movie of yourself in action as if you are watching from the stands OR as if you are actually doing it. Michael Phelps is known to have practiced both for all his races.**

Give it a try! Be sure to check out the other visualization resources and bonus material in the *Unstoppable Resource Training Room* online.

"TO GIVE ANYTHING
LESS THAN YOUR
BEST IS TO SACRIFICE
THE GIFT."

–STEVE PREFONTAINE

Those with a fixed mindset let failures define them. With a growth mindset, failures and setbacks are motivating. Researchers have found that mistakes are not only an opportunity for learning, they result in synapses firing in your brain, sparking growth. Making and learning from mistakes is the exercise your brain needs to keep growing!

With a growth mindset, you can look at mistakes, failures, and any day-to-day struggles in a new light. Sometimes as a result of a "failure" a new opportunity arises or it motivates you to do something you wouldn't have done otherwise. Didn't get into the college of your dreams? Maybe the one you are at is the best thing that ever happened to you. Didn't make the team you tried out for? Maybe the new sport you decided to try instead will bring you great joy.

Have you had an event that was initially a "failure" in your mind, but it turned out to open up new doors, connect you with others, or motivate you in a way you wouldn't have felt before? You can change your mind and the way you look at failures.

> ## "SUCCESS IS NEVER FINAL, FAILURE IS NEVER FATAL. IT'S COURAGE THAT COUNTS."
>
> –JOHN WOODEN

MICHAEL JORDAN GOT CUT FROM HIS HIGH SCHOOL'S VARSITY BASKETBALL TEAM BUT HE DIDN'T QUIT.

WILMA RUDOLPH WAS TOLD SHE'D NEVER WALK AGAIN AFTER AN INFANT CASE OF POLIO BUT BECAME THE FASTEST WOMAN IN THE WORLD IN 1960.

THEODOR GEISEL, KNOWN AS "DR. SEUSS", GOT HIS FIRST MANUSCRIPT REJECTED BY 27 PUBLISHERS.

THE MICROWAVE WAS MADE BY MISTAKE WHILE PERCY SPENCER WAS WORKING ON A RADAR SET AND HE NOTICED A CHOCOLATE BAR IN HIS POCKET WAS MELTING.

POST-IT NOTES WERE CREATED WHEN TRYING TO ACTUALLY MAKE A SUPER STRONG ADHESIVE.

WHAT IS YOUR "FAVORITE FAILURE"?

"I'VE MISSED MORE THAN 9,000 SHOTS IN MY CAREER. I'VE LOST ALMOST 300 GAMES. TWENTY SIX TIMES I'VE BEEN TRUSTED TO TAKE THE GAME WINNING SHOT AND MISSED. I'VE FAILED OVER AND OVER AND OVER AGAIN IN MY LIFE. AND THAT IS WHY I SUCCEED."

-MICHAEL JORDAN

THE POWER OF YET

What are some specific skills that you WANT to do in your sport or performance but are unable to do....YET

NEED TO CHANGE FROM A FIXED MINDSET TO A GROWTH MINDSET? TRY THIS:

‣ Practice mindfulness (Huddle 6) and growing your awareness around your word choices, thoughts, and the voice you use both externally and internally.

‣ When you notice a fixed mindset voice, talk back to it with growth mindset language (and practice doing this for others when you hear their fixed mindset voice!). Knowing you have the choice in how you respond to events and think about them can be quite helpful.

‣ When you notice using your growth mindset voice, pat yourself on the back and celebrate it!

‣ Choose to act on and believe the growth mindset voice.

More information and resources from Carol Dweck and her team can be found at:
www.mindsetonline.com

THINK
CONFIDENT

What do Michael Jordan, Wilma Rudolph, Walt Disney, and Dr. Seuss have in common? A combination of a growth mindset, the belief in the ability to continue to grow and improve through effort and hard work, and self-efficacy. With a growth mindset you take responsibility and get busy. You don't make excuses or leave your fate to talent alone.

CONFIDENCE & SELF-EFFICACY

Confidence is a belief in your own abilities and strengths. Developing your confidence helps you try new things, cope with challenges and mistakes, and take pride in your abilities and accomplishments. Confidence can come as a result of how you think and what you focus on. Self-efficacy is a situation specific type of confidence – the belief or expectation that you will succeed at a particular task or challenge. There is a strong link between self-efficacy and performance.

Both self-efficacy and self-confidence are important components of building mental toughness. **You can own that and change it**.

Many people believe that confidence is a feeling. *I don't feel confident.* Instead, it is a belief. If confidence is a *belief,* that means it's a *thought.* If confidence is a *thought,* that means you own that and can change it!

START BELIEVING AND THINKING CONFIDENTLY, RATHER THAN WAITING TO FEEL IT.

SELF-TALK

Some studies have shown you have up to **60,000 thoughts** per day. We all engage in an internal dialogue with ourselves daily. That internal dialogue is sometimes referred to as self-talk. Self-talk is also considered the most tried and true way for increasing your self-confidence. You, too, can learn to talk to yourself in positive and productive ways.

Remember, it's about *thinking* confidently. So, it is important to be aware of what your self-talk is like.

Fill in some more examples below:

THE EVENT (IF APPLICABLE)	NEGATIVE THOUGHTS	NEW THOUGHT (CAN YOU REFRAME IT INTO A MORE CONSTRUCTIVE WAY?)
i.e. practice	"I hate practicing in the cold weather."	Ex1: "It can't be perfect weather all the time." Ex 2: "I love my teammates and the chance to play." Ex 3: "I like having a break from doing homework."

Now is your opportunity to create your "go-to" statement for performance, one that you say to yourself before and during practice AND competition. You can make it part of your routine.

Examples: "Swish." (basketball); "Relax and breathe."; "Just breathe"; ….

MY SELF-TALK PERFORMANCE STATEMENT:

Consider also having a statement to write on the top of your tests. "I'm prepared for this." "I got this!" "I'm unstoppable!" "I'm ready for this.", etc. A statement should never be about the outcome and should be empowering.

Let's take it one step further. Rather than wishing friends luck in competition or for assessments, consider giving a much more empowering statement. What are some alternates to saying, "good luck!"?

CHALK
TALK SPOT
GOOD LUCK? NOPE, IT'S
HARD WORK, NOT
LUCK.

Examples: *Have fun. You got this! Do your thing!*

GIVE YOURSELF A
BOOST IN CONFIDENCE

From The Champions Comeback by Jim Afremow, here are eight strategies for boosting your confidence. You can try them and see what works for you.

1 Give yourself a mental high five after executing a play or performance as planned. Positive self-reinforcement is like making a deposit in your confidence account.

2 Reflect on your past successes and highlights. This will lead to better play in the future. Replay these magic moments in your mind and feel how good they felt at the time. Later, when you need an extra boost, it will be easier to draw on these feelings.

3 Remember a particular occasion when you triumphed over a difficult challenge, such as overcoming fear in the face of a tryout or bouncing back from an injury. Write down some of the keys that made this success possible.

4 Think about the compliments others have paid you and your abilities. Remember what teammates, friends, coaches, and family members have said about your athletic prowess. They are the ones that know you and what you are capable of.

5 Mirror and mimic what your role models did to become champions.

6 Stand in a confident posture—feet apart, chin up, chest out, with a broad smile.

7 Repeat this to yourself prior to a competition: "I've practiced and I trust my training and preparation."

8 During key moments of a performance, command yourself to "Believe in yourself!"

THOUGHTS
ARE NOT
FACTS

Thoughts are not facts. You can choose what thoughts to listen to.

You will not always be able to prevent negative thoughts coming into your mind. Too often, we listen to those negative thoughts. Here's the trick, you must understand <u>your thoughts don't have to impact your actions.</u>

WE DON'T HAVE TO BELIEVE THEM.

CHALK
TALK SPOT
"I DONT HAVE TO BELIEVE MY THOUGHTS." REPEAT THAT!

Say "I can't tap my hand" while tapping your hand. Think about this for a second! Your thoughts don't have to impact your actions. You are, in fact, tapping your hand, in SPITE of that thought!

While thinking confidently is icing on the cake and what you strive for, you don't have to be confident to perform well. All athletes have had days they felt bad and performed well and days they felt good and performed poorly. While there is a lot of research that shows a direct correlation between self-confidence and success, it's not the only path to peak performance. Mindfulness training in Huddle 6 can help with strategies for understanding how negative thoughts and feelings can arise and we can still perform well.

THIS WEEK'S INTENTION IN ONE WORD:

. . . .

THOUGHT I HAVE HAD THAT I WILL CHOOSE NOT TO BELIEVE:

. . . .

. . . .

DATE   WORKOUT/PLAN/FOCUS:

MON

TODAY'S **SPEC**:

TUES

TODAY'S **SPEC**:

WED

TODAY'S **SPEC**:

Reminder: Your daily **SPEC** is a **s**mall **p**ositive, **e**njoyable, and/or **c**ool thing from your day!

WORKOUT/PLAN/FOCUS   DATE

THU

TODAY'S **SPEC**:

FRI

TODAY'S **SPEC**:

SAT

TODAY'S **SPEC**:

SUN

TODAY'S **SPEC**:

"NINETY PERCENT OF THE GAME IS HALF MENTAL."
—YOGI BERRA

ZOOMING IN

| Creativity | Curiousity | Judgement | Perspective | Bravery | Perseverance |

| Zest | Honesty | Social Intelligence | Kindness | Love | Leadership |

WHAT WENT WELL this week in performance (or practice/training, if applicable)?

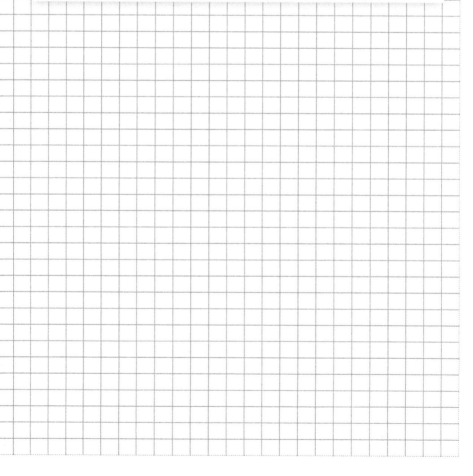

ON YOUR STRENGTHS...

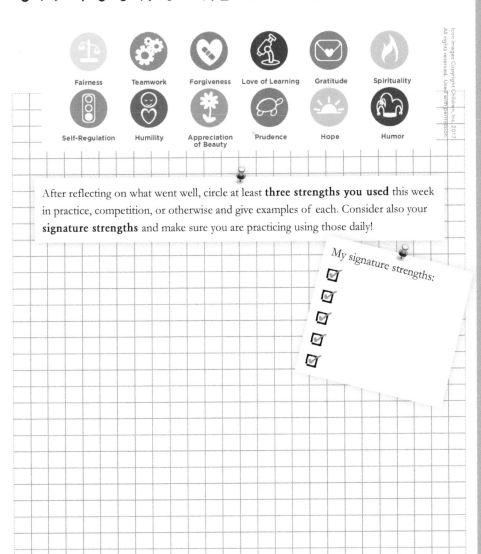

Fairness · Teamwork · Forgiveness · Love of Learning · Gratitude · Spirituality

Self-Regulation · Humility · Appreciation of Beauty · Prudence · Hope · Humor

After reflecting on what went well, circle at least **three strengths you used** this week in practice, competition, or otherwise and give examples of each. Consider also your **signature strengths** and make sure you are practicing using those daily!

My signature strengths:

☑

☑

☑

☑

☑

TIME FOR T.W.C.

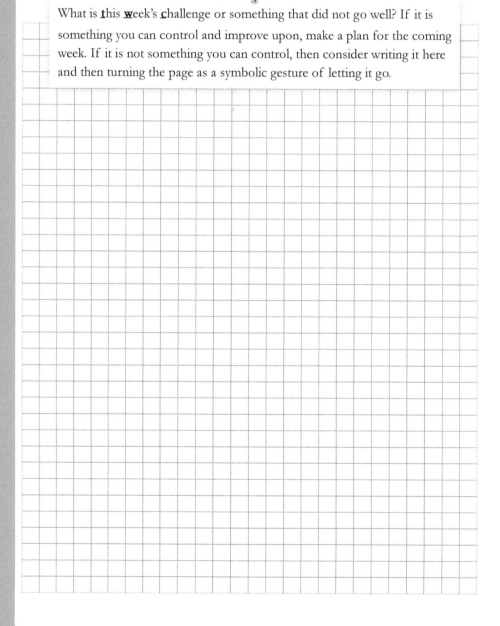

What is this week's challenge or something that did not go well? If it is something you can control and improve upon, make a plan for the coming week. If it is not something you can control, then consider writing it here and then turning the page as a symbolic gesture of letting it go.

CHECK IN... HOW ARE YOU DOING BALANCING YOUR PLATE <u>DAILY</u>?

Refer to page 30 if you need a refresher

☐ SLEEP   ☐ NUTRITION

☐ PHYSICAL ACTIVITY TIME

☐ CONNECTION/ SOCIAL TIME

☐ REFLECTION TIME

☐ MENTAL RECOVERY TIME
(DOWNTIME/GOOD GOOFING OFF)

What steps will you take to make sure each of these essential elements are part of your upcoming week?

HUDDLE 4

VISION

"CHAMPIONS AREN'T MADE IN THE GYMS. CHAMPIONS ARE MADE FROM SOMETHING THEY HAVE DEEP INSIDE THEM — A DESIRE, A DREAM, A VISION."

MUHAMMAD ALI

HUDDLE 4
VISION

IN THIS HUDDLE:

▷ What are my inspirational values?

▷ How do I hope to be remembered as an athlete and on this team?

▷ What is the SMARTY goal setting principle and how can I set goals?

▷ What is the WOOP mental strategy that can help me overcome obstacles and reach my goals?

Your vision muscle can be developed by identifying your values and setting your goals. Values are part of your road map for how you want to be in a situation, practice, or performance (no matter what the outcome) versus goals which are achievable (outcome oriented).

To really thrive in whatever it is you are doing (school, sports, music, etc.), you must value what you're doing. You can and should be driven by your values.

When the alarm goes off and you don't feel like getting up and going to your morning practice, your motivating values are what push you through.

Because the reality is you have a choice in that moment, either keep sleeping and skip practice, or get up and go.

Some people might first think, "No way. I don't have a choice. I have to go to practice or else ___[fill in the blank]___." Wrong. You are still making a choice. You just have to understand that there may be consequences for your choice one way or the other.

This is true for just about everything you do. You don't "have" to go to the club meeting scheduled tonight. You might value the experience, the leadership opportunity, the fact that other people are counting on you, and you want to follow through with commitments, and that is why you go.

You can change the language you use and move away from the "have-tos" and toward "choose-tos." It can help you define your values and live in accordance with those values. By living in this way, you strengthen your ability to perform and to do your thing no matter what comes your way in that moment.

The following exercises can become an important and powerful tool for you. When you are burned out, not wanting to go to practice, coming back from an injury, not wanting to study for that math test, or deciding between going to a party or getting extra sleep the night before your game, having your values defined can inspire you to push forward and remind you of why you do it.

105

Who inspires you?

What inspires you?

What do you love about your
sport or performance realm?

Your life has meaning outside
your performance. What matters
to you and is important regardless
of outcomes?

Adapted from Amy Baltzell's *Living in the Sweet Spot* (2013)

"THE FUTURE NEVER JUST HAPPENED. IT WAS CREATED."

–MAE JEMISON

PARTY!

Imagine you are attending a party in honor of your retirement from your sport. Everyone in attendance knows you and/or watched you play. This includes your family, friends, coaches, former teammates, managers, referees and timers, athletic trainers, and everyone against whom you competed. The floor is open for each person to say something about you, your character, and how you competed. What would you like them to say about you?

"IT'S NOT HARD TO MAKE DECISIONS ONCE YOU KNOW WHAT YOUR VALUES ARE."

-ROY E. DISNEY

VALUES CHALLENGE

Take the bracket challenge as a way to help you prioritize and identify the values you MOST care about. You may find you can clearly identify your top values without going through this process, or it may be a process that just gets you thinking.

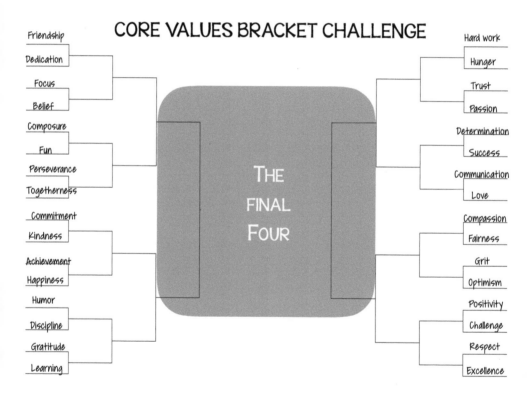

CORE VALUES BRACKET CHALLENGE

Friendship
Dedication
Focus
Belief
Composure
Fun
Perseverance
Togetherness
Commitment
Kindness
Achievement
Happiness
Humor
Discipline
Gratitude
Learning

THE FINAL FOUR

Hard work
Hunger
Trust
Passion
Determination
Success
Communication
Love
Compassion
Fairness
Grit
Optimism
Positivity
Challenge
Respect
Excellence

Think about the last few exercises. What and who inspires you?; Your perspective; What you want people to say about you at your retirement party?; and your personal values bracket. List your top four values here and define what they mean to you in your own words.

_____ :

_____ :

_____ :

_____ :

"SET LOFTY GOALS FOR YOURSELF AND BELIEVE THAT WITH REALLY HARD WORK YOU CAN ACHIEVE THEM."

-IBTIHAJ MUHAMMAD

SET
GOALS

Now that you have defined your values, it is time to consider setting goals. Goal setting has been shown to influence the performance of athletes and has also been linked to positive changes in psychological states such as anxiety, confidence, and motivation. It is an extremely powerful technique for enhancing performance, but it must be implemented properly.

To begin the process of setting your goals for the season, it is helpful to think in terms of the SMARTY principal (as defined in *Living in the Sweet Spot* by Amy Baltzell). What are the SMARTY principals?

Why is the YOU in SMARTY so important?

S SPECIFIC— For example, rather than I want to get in better shape" one might say My goal is to go to the gym two times a week."

M MEASURABLE— For example, I want to run two miles three days a week. For goals that are less obviously measurable, such as I want to enjoy practice more," you can use a scale from zero to ten for where you want to be.

A ADJUSTABLE— For example, if you are running five miles a day and you realize your body is in pain, you may need to adjust your mileage.

R REALISTIC— Challenging, but not too challenging

T TIME SENSITIVE— So you can really focus your energy and measure your progress. Think of goals for <u>this season</u> or for this pre-season.

Y YOU— Goals should matter to <u>you</u>. You have to value your goals authentically and genuinely, and you must realistically want to achieve them yourself.

There are two types of motivation: intrinsic and extrinsic. Intrinsic motivation is when you do something because you inherently want to or enjoy it. Extrinsic motivation is doing something for rewards or because you get something out of it. Studies continue to show that when you mainly value the rewards you get for doing a task, you lose your inherent interest in doing the task. So when you set your goals and take steps to reach them, keep your inspired values in mind and make sure your goal matters to <u>you</u>.

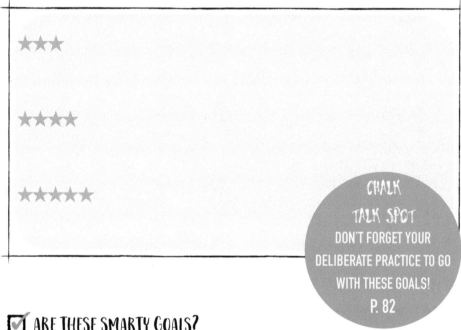

A SMARTY
SEASON

STAR PERFORMANCE GOALS:

Based on your current skill level, your current motivation, and your commitment to focus on improvement and deliberate practice, what are realistic performance goals for the season? Identify a 3 star goal, a 4 star goal, and a 5 star goal (5 star being the biggest stretch and reach for you).

★★★

★★★★

★★★★★

CHALK TALK SPOT
DON'T FORGET YOUR DELIBERATE PRACTICE TO GO WITH THESE GOALS!
P. 82

☑ ARE THESE SMARTY GOALS?

☐ **S**pecific

☐ **M**easurable

☐ **A**djustable

☐ **R**ealistic

☐ **T**ime-Sensitive

☐ **Y**ou (Important to **me**)

PRACTICE GOALS

Name your practice goals for your upcoming practices. Common practice goals may include focusing 100 percent, making five positive statements to teammates, running to and from all drills, etc.

☑ ARE THESE SMARTY GOALS?

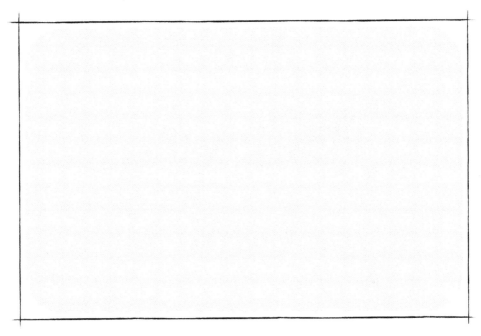

- **S**pecific
- **M**easurable
- **A**djustable
- **R**ealistic
- **T**ime-Sensitive
- **Y**ou (Important to **me**)

Interested in becoming world class? You need more than SMARTY goals. You need a HUGG. What are HUGGs? Andy Cope, founder of The Art of Brilliance and renowned author, describes a HUGG as a:

HUGE

UNBELIEVABLY

GREAT

GOAL

Set your HUGG and then work your way through the pyramid on the page to the right to identify the steps necessary to help you reach your goal, right down to the habits of today. Consider not only the skills you may need, but also the everyday leadership you exhibit to reach your goal, such as surrounding yourself with the right people, doing well in school, etc.

WORLD CLASS GOALS

Fill in the HUGG pyramid!

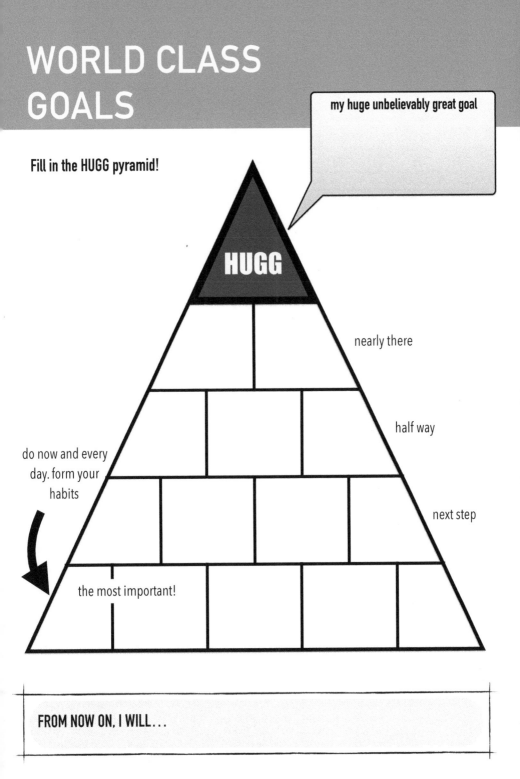

my huge unbelievably great goal

HUGG

nearly there

half way

do now and every day. form your habits

next step

the most important!

FROM NOW ON, I WILL...

"IT'S BETTER TO LOOK AHEAD AND PREPARE THAN TO LOOK BACK AND REGRET."

-JACKIE JOYNER-KERSEE

GOAL OF SELF LOVE

Remember that your life has meaning outside of your performance. You are a worthy and valued human being regardless of whether or not you achieve your performance goal(s) or any particular outcomes. What commitment can you make to breed self-acceptance?

"OBSTACLES AREN'T THERE TO STOP YOU. THEY ARE PUT THERE TO SHOW YOU HOW POWERFUL YOU CAN FEEL WHEN YOU RUN RIGHT OVER THEM."

–MARTYN ROONEY

WOOP IT!

WOOP MENTAL STRATEGY

One strategy to consider when setting your goal, big or small (in or outside of your sport), involves what scientists call "mental contrasting" the future and the reality.

Professor and researcher Gabriele Oettingen, author of *Rethinking Positive Thinking* developed mental contrasting and a method called WOOP (short for Wish, Outcome, Obstacle, Plan). This strategy builds self-control — something most athletes want. WOOP helps you dream about the future (realistically) but also identify and imagine what inner obstacle may prevent you from achieving your dreams. Once identifying this obstacle, you make a plan for how to overcome it. (This is scientifically known as *implementation intentions*, a strategy discovered by Prof. Peter M. Gollwitzer).

Incorporating the WOOP principles into your goal setting helps you plan ahead for what inner obstacles you might face. You identify your inner obstacle and make the plan now, rather than in the moment when the obstacle presents itself and is often hard to think clearly. Combine this with having a SMARTY goal (one that is specific, measurable, adjustable, realistic, measurable, and matters to you), and you have a great plan for tackling your season and making your wishes come true. By using the WOOP strategy, you will visualize the outcome you desire and also visualize the obstacles that might stand in your way.

CHALK TALK SPOT
GO TO THE ONLINE COURSE AND
PRACTICE ONE OF THE SIX
BREATHING TECHNIQUES!

Here is what each of the letters stand for in WOOP:

W   WISH— A wish is something you want to accomplish. Something challenging, but realistic and important to you. Perhaps your SMARTY goal!

     i.e. I would like to get 8 hours of sleep every night."

O   OUTCOME — Identify the best result or feeling from accomplishing your goal. Visualize this outcome.

     i.e. I would feel alert."

O   OBSTACLE —The personal/inner obstacle that may prevent you from accomplishing your goal. It could be an emotion, an irrational belief, or a bad habit.

     i.e. I get distracted by Netflix and Snapchat."

P   PLAN — If_____[obstacle happens], then I will _____[action to overcome obstacle].

     i.e. If/When I get distracted by Netflix and Snapchat, I will turn it off to complete my homework and go to bed.

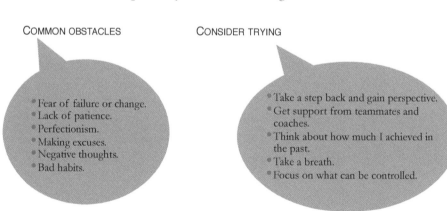

COMMON OBSTACLES

- Fear of failure or change.
- Lack of patience.
- Perfectionism.
- Making excuses.
- Negative thoughts.
- Bad habits.

CONSIDER TRYING

- Take a step back and gain perspective.
- Get support from teammates and coaches.
- Think about how much I achieved in the past.
- Take a breath.
- Focus on what can be controlled.

Beyond what you read here, more information about the science and details of WOOP can be found at woopmylife.org or characterlab.org/woop. There is also the WOOP app that can help you become a woop-expert.

"THE SECRET TO GETTING AHEAD IS GETTING STARTED."

–MARK TWAIN

WELLNESS WISH

This wish is for health, sleep, nutrition, etc. Keep SMARTY in mind. Don't just say "sleep more." Instead, perhaps say "Be in bed with no technology by 11pm each night." or "Eat breakfast every day." What is your wellness wish for your season? Consider something that is challenging but realistic.

OUTCOME:

Visualize this!

INNER OBSTACLE:

Something in your control.
Visualize this!

PLAN:

IF_____ I WILL_____
        [Obstacle]   [Action]

SMALL GOALS

Throughout the year, come back to this page if there are small wishes or goals you want to accomplish in or outside of your sport.

Need to finish that term paper? WOOP it.

Want to meditate ten minutes every day? WOOP it.

Want to eat breakfast every morning before class? WOOP it.

Want to stop procrastinating your work? WOOP it.

Want to lift three days a week? WOOP it.

Want to watch less Netflix and spend more time with friends? WOOP it.

You can WOOP anything!

CHALK TALK SPOT
LIVE BY YOUR VALUES. WHAT ARE THOSE CORE VALUES OWNED AND OPERATED BY YOU?

WISH:

OUTCOME:

OBSTACLE:

PLAN:

IF_____ I WILL_____

MY <u>DREAM</u> GOAL (SPORT OR NOT SPORT RELATED) IF ALL BARRIERS WERE LIFTED:

....

....

DATE   WORKOUT/PLAN/FOCUS

MON

TODAY'S **SPEC**:

TUES

TODAY'S **SPEC**:

WED

TODAY'S **SPEC**:

Reminder: Your daily **SPEC** is a <u>s</u>mall <u>p</u>ositive, <u>e</u>njoyable, and/or <u>c</u>ool thing from your day!

WORKOUT/PLAN/FOCUS   DATE

THU

TODAY'S **SPEC**:

FRI

TODAY'S **SPEC**:

SAT

TODAY'S **SPEC**:

SUN

TODAY'S **SPEC**:

"EACH OF US HAS A FIRE IN OUR HEARTS FOR SOMETHING. IT'S OUR
GOAL IN LIFE TO FIND IT AND KEEP IT LIT."
—MARY LOU RETTON

ZOOMING IN

Creativity · Curiousity · Judgement · Perspective · Bravery · Perseverance

Zest · Honesty · Social Intelligence · Kindness · Love · Leadership

WHAT WENT WELL this week in performance (or practice/training, if applicable)?

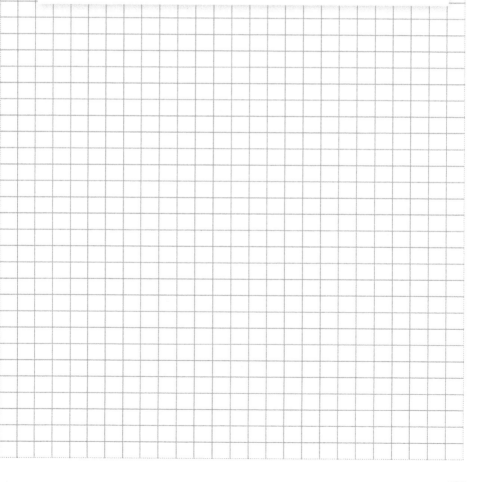

ON YOUR STRENGTHS...

| Fairness | Teamwork | Forgiveness | Love of Learning | Gratitude | Spirituality |

| Self-Regulation | Humility | Appreciation of Beauty | Prudence | Hope | Humor |

After reflecting on what went well, circle at least **three strengths you used** this week in practice, competition, or otherwise and give examples of each. Consider also your **signature strengths** and make sure you are practicing using those daily!

My signature strengths:

☑

☑

☑

☑

☑

TIME FOR T.W.C.

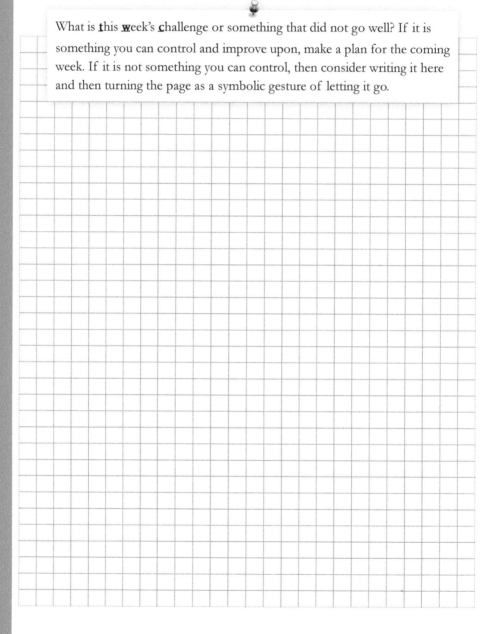

What is **t**his **w**eek's **c**hallenge or something that did not go well? If it is something you can control and improve upon, make a plan for the coming week. If it is not something you can control, then consider writing it here and then turning the page as a symbolic gesture of letting it go.

CHECK IN... HOW ARE YOU DOING BALANCING YOUR PLATE <u>DAILY</u>?

Refer to page 30 if you need a refresher

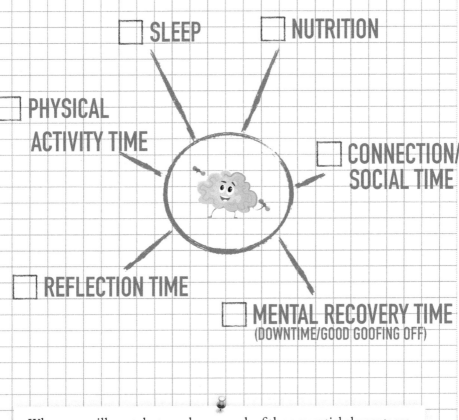

☐ SLEEP   ☐ NUTRITION

☐ PHYSICAL ACTIVITY TIME

☐ CONNECTION/ SOCIAL TIME

☐ REFLECTION TIME

☐ MENTAL RECOVERY TIME
(DOWNTIME/GOOD GOOFING OFF)

What steps will you take to make sure each of these essential elements are part of your upcoming week?

HUDDLE 5

GRATITUDE

"GRATITUDE IS LOOKING ON THE BRIGHTER SIDE OF LIFE, EVEN IF IT MEANS HURTING YOUR EYES."

- ELLEN DEGENERES

HUDDLE 5
GRATITUDE

IN THIS HUDDLE:
▷ What does gratitude have to do with my performance?
▷ Who are the people involved in allowing me to do my thing and perform daily?
▷ What moments (past, present, or future) can I savor with respect to my season?

You have total control over building your gratitude muscle daily. Gratitude helps build a positive perspective, one that allows you to think big picture while also focusing on the moment, especially in high pressure situations. This perspective also allows you to better tolerate and even enjoy the day-to-day grind in practice, performance, or life in general while also stretching yourself.

Gratitude is like a muscle that needs to be exercised and strengthened. The more you practice it, the more it becomes effortless and part of your being. It simply becomes who you are and how you see the world.

Think about some behaviors that are automatic. Maybe you always say thank you at the end of a check-out line at the grocery store, but don't even really think about it anymore, you just do it. Maybe starting your car is automatic. You may have to put your foot on the break to turn the engine over, and at one time you probably had to think about it, but now perhaps it just happens. These are examples of things you had to once pay attention to and practice and eventually

they became fairly effortless and just part of what you do. The point is, spend time focusing on practicing and building your gratitude muscle and soon this perspective will be part of you.

Why is it worth it? Study after study shows that practicing gratitude reduces stress and increases happiness and well-being. Research also shows that gratitude helps you recover quicker from illness or injuries, have better health, exercise more, feel more optimistic, and think more clearly under pressure. Each of these outcomes can have a direct and positive effect on performance. Some studies have shown that writing three things you are grateful for each night or writing five gratitude statements each week can have significant beneficial impacts on your life. The point is, bringing greater awareness to the good happening on an ongoing basis does your body and mind good. From this point forward you will have a spot in the weekly calendar section to write 5 gratitudes from your week. Consider this and your daily SPEC to be very important parts of your mental training!

135

"WE MUST FIND TIME
TO STOP AND THANK THE
PEOPLE WHO MAKE A
DIFFERENCE IN OUR
LIVES."

-JOHN F. KENNEDY

SAY
THANK YOU

THANK YOU LETTERS

Make a list below of all the people you can think of from the past and/or present that help/allow you do what you do. (e.g. custodians, laundry staff, scheduling officer, athletic director, coaches, parents, teachers, teammates, the staff that mow the grass on your field or paint the lines for your team, athletic trainers, etc.)

☐ _____   ☐ _____
☐ _____   ☐ _____
☐ _____   ☐ _____
☐ _____   ☐ _____
☐ _____   ☐ _____
☐ _____   ☐ _____
☐ _____   ☐ _____
☐ _____   ☐ _____
☐ _____   ☐ _____
☐ _____   ☐ _____
☐ _____   ☐ _____
☐ _____   ☐ _____

Set aside some time to write gratitude cards to the people you have listed above. Then deliver them in person or mail them and check them off from your list.

DID YOU KNOW?
IT'S PHYSIOLOGICALLY IMPOSSIBLE TO FEEL STRESS AND BE THANKFUL AT THE SAME TIME.

My super big ongoing gratitude list:

"NO MATTER WHAT
ACCOMPLISHMENTS
YOU MAKE, SOMEBODY
HELPS YOU."

–WILMA RUDOLPH

REMIND YOURSELF WHAT YOU LOVE

THINGS THAT I AM GRATEFUL FOR AND ENJOY ABOUT TRAINING/PRACTICE:

e.g. Stretching, keeping a training journal, watching video, lifting weights, running, visualizing best performances

1.

2.

3.

Even when I am tired, frustrated, or didn't perform at my best, I am still grateful for and/or love:

4.

5.

6.

THINGS THAT I AM GRATEFUL FOR AND ENJOY ABOUT COMPETITION/PERFORMANCE:

e.g. The energy of the crowd, the reality that you are so prepared, the chance to see how well you can do, etc.

1.

2.

3.

Even when I am tired, frustrated, or didn't perform at my best, I am still grateful for and/or love:

4.

5.

6.

Adapted from Amy Baltzell's *Living in the Sweet Spot* (2013)

YOUR BANK ACCOUNT
OF GOODNESS

SAVORING

Now that you have moments, even small moments, of gratitude and awesomeness, take time to savor them. Savoring is noticing and appreciating the positive aspects of your life. Researcher Lea Waters, author of *The Strength Switch*, describes savoring like creating a "bank account of goodness." You can draw from your bank during difficult times.

Waters notes four main ways to practice savoring: **1)** Noticing the environment (waves crashing, the breeze on a hot summer day, the crisp air for your morning run, the sun, a rainbow, etc.); **2)** Noticing sensations (such as the smell of your favorite cookies, the taste of water to quench your thirst, etc.); **3)** recalling past moments (a game or activity you loved); and, **4)** Looking ahead to something happening in the future (such as looking forward to a trip, vacation, seeing your family, etc.).

What are things in your practice or performance environment that captivate your attention? Walking onto the field? The sight of the crowd?

What are smells, sounds, or physical sensations in practice or performance that capture your attention? The sound of the crowd? The feeling of a full-on sweat? The smell of a run through the woods?

Think back on your season (or year) thus far. What is a moment from the season, practice or competition that you'd like to savor?

What is something good you have planned for the future that you are looking forward to?

My ongoing list of moments to savor:

CHALK TALK SPOT

TRY THIS: WALK BETWEEN CLASSES (OR ANYWHERE PUBLIC) <u>BY YOURSELF</u> AND GET FROM POINT A TO POINT B WITHOUT LOOKING AT YOUR PHONE. OBSERVE YOUR SURROUNDINGS. SMILE AT STRANGERS. YOU ARE BUILDING YOUR MINDFULNESS MUSCLE!

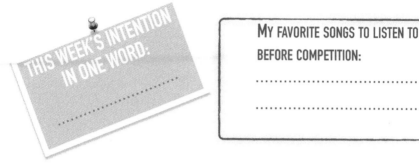

THIS WEEK'S INTENTION IN ONE WORD:

....

MY FAVORITE SONGS TO LISTEN TO
BEFORE COMPETITION:

....

....

DATE   WORKOUT/PLAN/FOCUS

MON

TODAY'S **SPEC**:

TUES

TODAY'S **SPEC**:

WED

TODAY'S **SPEC**:

Now is another good check point to see if you need to make another Tiny Habits® recipe (page 29) for yourself. How can you cultivate more gratitude practices daily or weekly?

After _____, I will _____ and I will reward myself by _____

    [prompt]   [a practice of gratitude]   [my celebration!]

WORKOUT/PLAN/FOCUS

DATE

THU

TODAY'S **SPEC**:

FRI

TODAY'S **SPEC**:

SAT

TODAY'S **SPEC**:

SUN

TODAY'S **SPEC**:

5 GRATITUDES FROM THE WEEK:

145

ZOOMING IN

Creativity

Curiousity

Judgement

Perspective

Bravery

Perseverance

Zest

Honesty

Social Intelligence

Kindness

Love

Leadership

WHAT WENT WELL this week in performance (or practice/training, if applicable)?

ON YOUR STRENGTHS...

Fairness

Teamwork

Forgiveness

Love of Learning

Gratitude

Spirituality

Self-Regulation

Humility

Appreciation of Beauty

Prudence

Hope

Humor

After reflecting on what went well, circle at least **three strengths you used** this week in practice, competition, or otherwise and give examples of each. Consider also your **signature strengths** and make sure you are practicing using those daily!

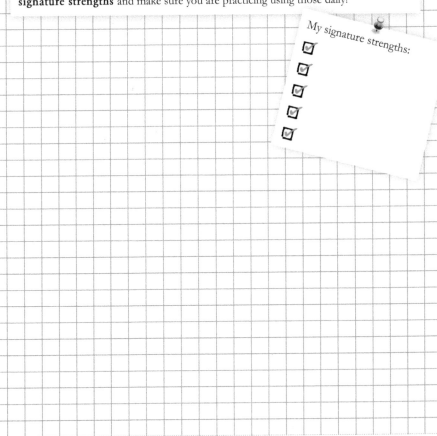

My signature strengths:

☑
☑
☑
☑
☑

TIME FOR T.W.C.

What is this week's challenge or something that did not go well? If it is something you can control and improve upon, make a plan for the coming week. If it is not something you can control, then consider writing it here and then turning the page as a symbolic gesture of letting it go.

CHECK IN...HOW ARE YOU DOING BALANCING YOUR PLATE <u>DAILY?</u>

Refer to page 30 if you need a refresher

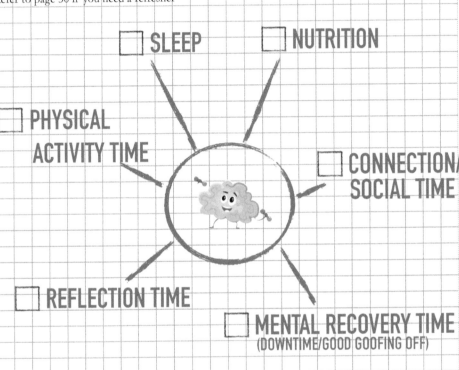

☐ SLEEP   ☐ NUTRITION

☐ PHYSICAL ACTIVITY TIME

☐ CONNECTION/ SOCIAL TIME

☐ REFLECTION TIME

☐ MENTAL RECOVERY TIME
(DOWNTIME/GOOD GOOFING OFF)

What steps will you take to make sure each of these essential elements are part of your upcoming week?

HUDDLE 6

MINDFULNESS & ATTENTION

"EVERY TIME I STEP
ON THE BASKETBALL
COURT, I NEVER KNOW
WHAT WILL HAPPEN. I
LIVE FOR THE
MOMENT. I PLAY FOR
THE MOMENT."

-MICHAEL JORDAN

HUDDLE 6
MINDFULNESS & ATTENTION

IN THIS HUDDLE:

▷ What is mindfulness and what does it have to do with performance?

▷ How can I build attention and block out distractions?

▷ How can I build a habit and practice mindfulness daily?

▷ How can I experience more performance states in flow?

Your mindfulness muscle is strengthened through continual practice. We face a number of modern day distractions, from cell phones to emails to thinking you can multi-task (which, by the way, brain research proves you can't) to your always growing list of things you must do within a 24-hour day. But the biggest distraction? Your own wandering mind.

Two things that can keep our mind from straying are **happiness** and **cognitive control**. Cognitive control is a fancy scientific term for the ability to put your attention where you want it.

Strengthening your mindfulness muscle will help you strengthen your attention muscle.

Before your mind goes to an image of a monk sitting in the lotus position in silence all day, let me try to explain mindfulness. Jon Kabat-Zinn, a pioneer in bringing mindfulness to Western culture, has defined mindfulness as "Paying attention in a particular way: on purpose, in the present moment, and non-judgmentally." Broadly speaking, mindfulness is a state of high quality attention which can be developed with practice. It's the ability to "live in the moment." Meditation, on the other hand, is a formal activity that you can do or practice to develop your mind and strengthen mindfulness.

YOUR CURRENCY

Mindfulness has been linked to better emotional regulation, body awareness, and social relationships. It's also has been shown to boost your immune system, increase the gray matter in your brain, and decrease emotional reactivity and fear. Additionally, it improves your ability to learn, strengthens your ability to pay attention, and provides a way to ignore distractions while focusing on the moment.

Mindfulness can lead you through a journey of personal transformation athletically and otherwise.

One thing we know for sure is that the mind seems to have a will of its own. **Attention** is undoubtedly something you need and are asked to have in multiple domains of your life. So, learning how to cultivate that is a worthy pursuit. In one of his lectures, Peter Haberl, a sport psychologist for the U.S. Olympic Committee, said "**Our mind is a thought producing factory. Our mind has a thief who steals attention. Attention is the currency for performance.**"

"ATTENTION IS THE CURRENCY FOR PERFORMANCE."

—Peter Haberl

Remember the essential elements of the human mind and body on page 30? "Good goofing off" was one of the needs.

Recent research has shown that attention is also built through rest and play. Dr. Lea Waters, Australian psychologist and author, calls this "deliberate play" or "good goofing off." The three characteristics of this are:

1. The activity is not passive—you are not being fed stimulus (that means we are not talking about flipping through Instagram or watching Netflix!).

2. The activity engages your mind in a way that simultaneously gives it free rein (think playing a fun game of pickup in the gym).

3. You're good enough at the activity that you don't focus too closely on the process or technique.

Examples include doing a puzzle, playing a game outside with friends, building something, tinkering in the local Makerspace, cooking a favorite recipe, reading, arts and crafts, bullet journaling, playing a pick-up game, etc.

The average adult or teenager is only able to achieve sustained attention for 20-35 minutes at a time. To perform at your best, you must learn to grow this attention muscle.

So, put the phones and computers away and find some good goofing off to do in between your deliberate practicing (Huddle 3).

What are some good goofing off activities you enjoy?

THREE MAIN BENEFITS OF MINDFULNESS WITH RESPECT TO ANY PERFORMANCE DOMAIN:

1 Training your mind to put your attention where you want it and be present (the currency!).

2 Learning to tolerate whatever thoughts and emotions (even negative ones!) arise and still do your thing.

3 Training your mind to notice the *new*.

FREE YOURSELF
TO BE PRESENT

> "BETWEEN STIMULUS AND RESPONSE THERE IS A SPACE. IN THAT SPACE IS OUR POWER TO CHOOSE OUR RESPONSE. IN OUR RESPONSE LIES OUR GROWTH AND OUR FREEDOM."

-VIKTOR FRANKL

Reading the quote above, it is in that "space" that Austrian neurologist and Holocaust survivor Viktor Frankl is talking about that you have real power, real choices in how you respond or react. If your mind is distracted by irrelevant thoughts and emotions, you step out of the present and then the moment for intelligent response is gone before you know it. To quiet the mind, try the following three step process.

STEP 1. **REDUCE JUDGEMENT.**

Do not label the experience, performance, or moment as "good" or "bad." Non-judgement also means less calculating, worrying, thinking, trying, and controlling.

STEP 2. **NOTICE & TALK BACK.**

When you notice your mind has gone to calculating, worrying, thinking, trying, controlling, and judging, acknowledge it. Say to yourself "Judging, I see you. I don't need you." Or, "Okay, I am trying too hard right now. Not necessary.", etc. Acknowledge the unhelpful feelings… Thank them for coming…Let them know thy aren't needed.

STEP 3. **GET BUSY ON THE PRESENT.**

Bring yourself back to the present moment. If you are on the sidelines, cheer your team on. If you are in the game, what should your next action be? If you are about to take off at the start line, take a breath. If you aren't sure how to come back to the present moment, remember that you always have your breath with you and can always come back to it.

"THE LESS TENSION
AND EFFORT, THE
FASTER AND MORE
POWERFUL YOU
WILL BE."

–BRUCE LEE

With a quiet mind, you experience a form of freedom. Often times the outcomes you may seek or find rewarding come naturally, but you aren't TRYING for them, they come as a byproduct. Judgements can also interfere with your performance. Judgement and attachment to negative results and mistakes often cause more disappointment, not the event or mistake itself. You want, instead, **non-judgmental present moment awareness** which can be developed through practicing mindfulness.

If simply sitting with your eyes closed meditating sounds too passive and difficult right now, here are a few other ways to practice mindfulness:

BRUSHING YOUR TEETH

When you brush your teeth, just brush your teeth. Notice what it feels like. Hear the sound it makes. When you notice your mind start thinking or planning or worrying, bring it back to your teeth.

TIE YOUR SHOES

Do you loop swoop and pull or do bunny ears? Don't think about where you are going, just keep attention on tying your shoes.

EATING

Practice mindful eating. One way to do this might be to put your utensil down after every bite. Make sure you fully chew and swallow before taking another bite. Taste your food. Notice the texture, etc.

WALKING

In between classes or going from one point to another, rather than taking your phone out, just walk. Notice your feet touching the ground one after another. When you notice your mind wandering, bring it back to just walking.

LISTENING

When in conversation with a friend or when your coach is talking, just listen. When you notice your mind start planning what you want to say, bring yourself back to listening intently.

MINDFUL PAUSE

Similar to the S.T.O.P. breath reset on the next page. Pause what you are doing. Take a breath. Think of a character strength you can bring forward to your next task. Then continue.

THE RESET

Use the following simple acronym and method to bring your mind and body into balance at any point during your day. This could be while taking a test, before getting on the ice for your game, while worrying about the future, when walking between classes, in between bites of food, or really any time!

S

Stop. Stop what you are doing.

T

Take a breath. Take a *proper* breath (or more than one if you'd like!). When you are on the go, using and remembering a formula is another way to help ensure you are, in fact, getting air into the diaphragm. One such formula is 6-2-7: Breathe in for six seconds, hold for two, breathe out for 7 seconds. For younger kids, a formula is 4-2-5: Breathe in for four seconds, hold for two, breathe out for 5 seconds. Perhaps you develop your own formula that works for you or you are able to take a proper breath simply by the way it feels (and from your practice from the previous page).

O

Observe. Observe what is happening around you including your own thoughts, emotions, and sensations. Maybe relaxing your shoulders or unclenching your jaw or relaxing tension in your forehead is what you need in that moment.

P

Proceed. Reconnect with your experience and proceed to respond more in-the-moment.

Adapted from Bob Stahl & Elisha Goldstein, *A Mindfulness-Based Stress Reduction Workbook* (New Harbinger, 2010).

5 THINGS MINDFUL ATHLETES DO

1 PLAY IN THE PRESENT
MOMENT AND HAVE
MORE EXPERIENCES IN
"FLOW"
(Full engagement keeps you
focused on whatever task is
most helpful in that
moment.)

2 FORGIVE THEIR
MISTAKES–BIG AND
SMALL
(Allows you to move on
quickly to the next play.)

3 MINIMIZE EXTERNAL
DISTRACTIONS
(The crowd or the pressure
to win the game does not
prevent you from
performing your best.)

4 REGULATE EMOTIONS
(You can experience an
official's unfavorable call or
a teammate's unhelpful
attitude and still
concentrate on what you can
control.)

5 SHOW COMPASSION TO
SELF AND OTHERS
(Consistently demonstrate
good sportsmanship and act
compassionately to your
teammates and yourself.)

MEDITATION

There are many forms of meditation practice. Internationally known meditation teacher, Jack Kornfield said in his book *Meditation for Beginners*, "A good meditation practice is any one that develops awareness or mindfulness of our body and our senses, of our mind and our heart." It doesn't matter which method you choose. What matters is that you practice it regularly. Like practicing your sport or the violin, it takes discipline and grows with persistence. The goal in practicing meditation is not to become the best meditator in the world. The goal is to bring greater mental clarity and well-being, which then carries with you into the world and allows you to be the best version of yourself. The goal is for it to become part of you, a way of being, that is with you always. Also, like how you may practice basketball and see improvement, you must continue to play to continue to reap the benefits of your practice. If you didn't shoot a basketball for 5 years or even 5 months, you cannot expect to pick it up with the same touch and have the same shooting percentage. With meditation, it is not something you "complete" and then you "have" mindfulness for the rest of your life. Rather, it is something you continue to practice. Once you start feeling and noticing the benefits of meditation, that is not the time to stop and think you have completed the task. **Keep going.**

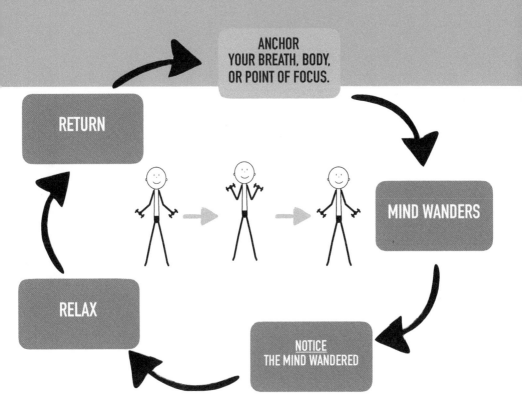

ANCHOR
YOUR BREATH, BODY,
OR POINT OF FOCUS.

RETURN

MIND WANDERS

RELAX

NOTICE
THE MIND WANDERED

Take a look at the meditation cycle above, as described to me by another internationally known meditation teacher, Josh Summers. Take special note of the "noticing" stage. As Josh described, to make the analogy to sports, that is where the reps happen. If you are working on your biceps you don't just hold the dumbbells. You curl them and there is a full range of motion that makes up one repetition. Meditation is not about a still mind where you think of nothing and are just at peace focusing on one thing. That is like holding the dumbbell without going through the full range of motion. You might have a variety of thoughts and emotions come to mind during a meditation. Like a weightlifting rep, each act of **noticing** builds skill in meditation and mindfulness. Here is your opportunity to practice positive self-talk and compassion, not judge yourself or label yourself as a "bad" meditator because your mind wandered. Just return your attention back to the point of focus.

CHALK
TALK SPOT
FIND A WAY TO MAKE
GROWING YOUR
MINDFULNESS MUSCLE A
HABIT!

ANOTHER MINDFUL WAY

Another approach comes from a particular type of mindfulness defined by Ellen Langer, social psychologist and professor at Harvard University. She describes mindfulness as achievable without meditation — it is "the simple act of actively noticing things." If someone asks me "How are you?" I have a pretty mindless response: "Good, thanks. How are you?" Langer has done a number of studies and argues it is *not* in this mindless, autopilot mode that we are at our best. It is when we mindfully engage, noticing subtle nuances and doing something distinctive that we enjoy ourselves more and perform better.

Instead of perceiving the world based on your past experiences, you can draw on novel distinctions. Be where you are. Right now. We'll sometimes get trapped in our own stories. Our tendency is to apply previously formed mindsets to current situations. This can diminish self-image and narrow our choices.

"We always lose to this team." "I always choke." "Coach doesn't like me me." "I don't test well." "I'm not a math person." "Practice is boring."

These are all comments that trap us in the past. Ellen Langer's approach to mindfulness, noticing the new in the situation, can help you get out of the trap.

> **TIP:**
> "BE WHERE YOUR FEET ARE" IS A COMMON MINDFULNESS MANTRA. AS AN ATHLETE, WHEN YOU SWITCH OUT OF YOUR SPIKES, CLEATS, OR SNEAKERS AFTER A GAME, CONSIDER THIS MOMENT A CHANCE TO BE WHERE YOUR FEET ARE. DON'T GET TOO TRAPPED INTO WHAT HAPPENED.

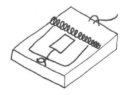

NOTICE
THE NEW

Late into a season, particularly, it is possible to become bored or disengaged. On the other hand, taking Langer's approach to mindfulness would allow you to walk into your home gym, rink, or field, a domain that you have stepped foot in hundreds if not thousands of times, and find something new. Maybe you look up into the stands and notice a sign that's different. Maybe you find the way your feet or shoes feel on the ground. The truth of the past doesn't have to influence the now. Find something new in the environment or internally in each practice or game. Bring something new with you to the event. Bringing your own touch of freshness might be enough to keep you engaged and with your attention where it best serves you for performance.

What are some possible new things to notice at practice or competitions this week (this could include attitudes, behavior, the breeze, sitting in a new spot to warmup, putting your stuff down in a different place, noticing something new in the physical practice space such as an item, sight, sound, lights, etc.)

Try noticing something new each and every day!

FLOW

There is another potential benefit to reducing distractions and encouraging mindfulness. Doing so can help you achieve the most productive form of focus and what many call "optimal performance" — the state of *flow*. Flow is experienced as a state of total but seemingly effortless focus. It is a state in which nothing but the activity at hand seems to matter in the moment. "In the zone." "He played out of his mind!" "I didn't feel pain or tired until the race was over." These are all comments you may have heard from people who have been lucky enough to experience a state of flow. Studies show that those who are more mindful are also more likely to experience a flow state.

Mihaly Csikzentmihalyi is the psychologist who coined the term and began studying flow in the 1970s. He is quoted as saying,

"THE HAPPIEST OF PEOPLE SPEND MUCH TIME IN A STATE OF FLOW, THE STATE IN WHICH PEOPLE ARE SO INVOLVED IN AN ACTIVITY THAT NOTHING ELSE SEEMS TO MATTER; THE EXPERIENCE ITSELF IS SO ENJOYABLE THAT PEOPLE WILL DO IT EVEN AT GREAT COST, FOR THE SHEER SAKE OF DOING IT."

It is not possible to force flow to happen. But you can lay a foundation that increases the likelihood of its occurrence. Mindfulness practice is one way to do that. Here are two more exercises to get you thinking about your past experiences in flow and a reminder for staying engaged in your performance.

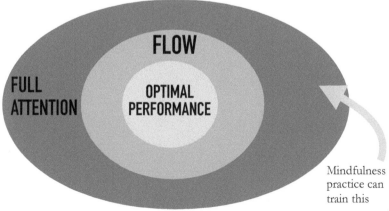

FLOW

FULL ATTENTION

OPTIMAL PERFORMANCE

Mindfulness practice can train this

YOUR EXPERIENCE
IN FLOW

Can you think back to a time when you experienced the state of flow in practice or performance? When you were fully engaged and nothing else really mattered? Perhaps when you felt time was distorted or as if no effort was really needed — it just happened. Was there an absence of negative thinking or worrying? How did your body feel?

Write about your experience below.

Adapted from Amy Baltzell's *Living in the Sweet Spot* (2013)

THE CHALLENGE

Flow most often happens when you feel skilled at the task while also doing something that challenges you. Finding joy in the challenge is a great step to set yourself up for more experiences in flow. The challenge can then absorb your attention and help you be fully engaged.

What do you love about practice when you are challenged? Focus on doing that as well as you can.

What do you love about competition when you are challenged? Remind yourself of this during tough times.

When are you most engaged in training?

What is your favorite part of your sport? Think back to when you were young and started playing. What do you love?

Adapted from *Living in the Sweet Spot* by Amy Baltzell (2013).

"DO YOU KNOW WHAT MY FAVORITE PART OF THE GAME IS? THE OPPORTUNITY TO PLAY."

— MIKE SINGLETARY

CHALK TALK SPOT
HOW ARE YOU SHOWING YOU ARE A LEADER?

MY IDEAL TIME TO GO TO BED:

....

....

DATE   WORKOUT/PLAN/FOCUS

MON

TODAY'S **SPEC**:

TUES

TODAY'S **SPEC**:

WED

TODAY'S **SPEC**:

Remember BJ Fogg's Tiny Habits® recipe (page 29)? Now would be a good time to make a plan for a meditation or mindfulness practice daily. Remember you can set a small habit so there is no excuse not to do it.:

After _____, I will _____ and I will reward myself by _____

    [prompt]   [my mindfulness habit]   [my celebration!]

WORKOUT/PLAN/FOCUS   DATE

THU

TODAY'S **SPEC**:

FRI

TODAY'S **SPEC**:

SAT

TODAY'S **SPEC**:

SUN

TODAY'S **SPEC**:

5 GRATITUDES FROM THE WEEK:

ZOOMING IN

Creativity

Curiousity

Judgement

Perspective

Bravery

Perseverance

Zest

Honesty

Social Intelligence

Kindness

Love

Leadership

WHAT WENT WELL this week in performance (or practice/training, if applicable)?

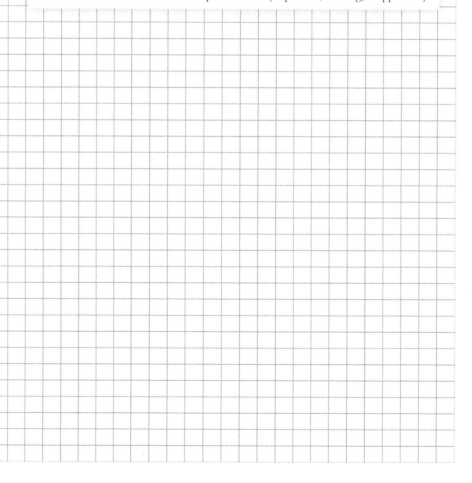

ON YOUR STRENGTHS...

| Fairness | Teamwork | Forgiveness | Love of Learning | Gratitude | Spirituality |

| Self-Regulation | Humility | Appreciation of Beauty | Prudence | Hope | Humor |

After reflecting on what went well, circle at least **three strengths you used** this week in practice, competition, or otherwise and give examples of each. Consider also your **signature strengths** and make sure you are practicing using those daily!

My signature strengths:
- ☑
- ☑
- ☑
- ☑
- ☑

TIME FOR T.W.C.

What is **t**his **w**eek's **c**hallenge or something that did not go well? If it is something you can control and improve upon, make a plan for the coming week. If it is not something you can control, then consider writing it here and then turning the page as a symbolic gesture of letting it go.

CHALK TALK SPOT
WHO HAVE YOU SAID, "THANK YOU" TO TODAY?

CHECK IN...HOW ARE YOU DOING BALANCING YOUR PLATE DAILY?

Refer to page 30 if you need a refresher

☐ SLEEP   ☐ NUTRITION

☐ PHYSICAL ACTIVITY TIME

☐ CONNECTION/ SOCIAL TIME

☐ REFLECTION TIME

☐ MENTAL RECOVERY TIME
(DOWNTIME/GOOD GOOFING OFF)

What steps will you take to make sure each of these essential elements are part of your upcoming week?

HUDDLE 7

COMPASSION

"WE MAY
ENCOUNTER MANY
DEFEATS BUT WE
MUST NOT BE
DEFEATED."

-MAYA ANGELOU

HUDDLE 7
COMPASSION

IN THIS HUDDLE:

▷ Don't I have to be self-critical in order to perform at my best and improve?

▷ How can I become the compassionate inner coach?

▷ How can I help foster a positive team environment through compassion for myself and for others?

To build your compassion muscle, it helps to focus both inwardly and outwardly. First, let's talk about what self-compassion means in sport. Self-compassion may even be the *ultimate* mental skill for building resilience, perseverance, reaching your goals, and **mental toughness**. Do you ever have any of the following thoughts?

I must criticize myself as a form of motivation. I aim to be the best, better than everyone else, and being not as good as others leaves me with a feeling of inadequacy. Social comparisons and competitions happen in my life. I judge myself (particularly in the midst of failure or mistakes). I avoid uncomfortable feelings. I experience self-doubt. I fear failure. I feel guilty when I don't perform up to my potential. I blame myself after losses in competition.

What if you had a tool to handle each of those moments? Self-compassion is the mental skill that gives you courage to face and tackle the difficult things in your life. Self-compassion is NOT being soft, making excuses for poor performance or blaming others. It is not self-indulgence (e.g., "I'm stressed out so I am going to watch Netflix all day."). It is not self-pity, when you become immersed in your own problems and forget that others have similar problems. It is also not self-esteem, your sense of self-worth or perceived value. Self-esteem often comes with the need to feel above average so your self-esteem may be high after successes and low after failures. It therefore isn't "there" for you when you need it most. Besides, how are we all supposed to be above average? It's impossible.

Dr. Kristin Neff is one of the leading experts on self-compassion, and she has really defined and conceptualized it for us, much like Carol Dweck conceptualized and defined the growth mindset.

THE THREE COMPONENTS OF SELF-COMPASSION

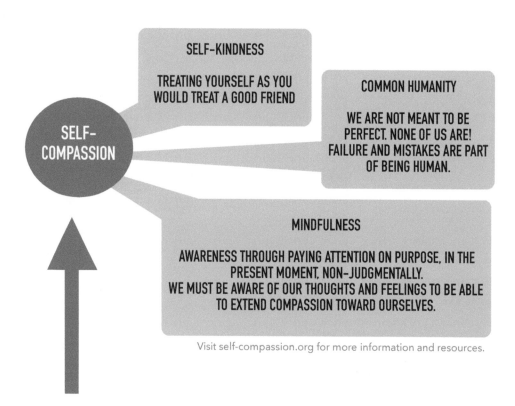

SELF-KINDNESS

TREATING YOURSELF AS YOU WOULD TREAT A GOOD FRIEND

SELF-COMPASSION

COMMON HUMANITY

WE ARE NOT MEANT TO BE PERFECT. NONE OF US ARE! FAILURE AND MISTAKES ARE PART OF BEING HUMAN.

MINDFULNESS

AWARENESS THROUGH PAYING ATTENTION ON PURPOSE, IN THE PRESENT MOMENT, NON-JUDGMENTALLY. WE MUST BE AWARE OF OUR THOUGHTS AND FEELINGS TO BE ABLE TO EXTEND COMPASSION TOWARD OURSELVES.

Visit self-compassion.org for more information and resources.

YOUR PATHWAY TO MENTAL TOUGHNESS

"EVERY STRIKE
BRINGS ME CLOSER TO
THE NEXT HOME RUN."

— BABE RUTH

While the norm for many athletes and high-achievers is to criticize themselves as a motivational tool, research shows that it can actually have a negative effect on peak performance.

If you watch some of the best athletes, they pick themselves up after mistakes. It is the quickest way to re-focus on what matters and perform at your best!

What does the research say about self-compassion and why does it matter for athletes?

- Self-compassion leads to greater intrinsic motivation (when you are driven by internal rewards).
- Self-compassion leads to being less afraid of failure which in turn will allow you to be more able to take on new challenges.
- Self-compassion leads to less rumination, less perfectionism, and lower levels of anxiety. This opens the space for your attention to be on what you <u>choose</u> for it to be on.
- Self-compassion allows you to be more willing to acknowledge negative emotions. With that, there is an understanding that emotions you feel don't have to impact how well you perform. Remember, you don't have to *feel* confident to perform well.
- Self-compassion is positively related to authentic pride, which motivates one to achieve higher performances.
- Self-compassion is linked to lower levels of self-criticism and less concern over mistakes, opening up pathways to increase resilience and progress toward your goals as well as the ability to move on quickly from mistakes and focus on the next play or the next action.
- Self-compassion can lead to more perseverance and the ability to get up (quickly!) after being knocked down. You can then get busy working toward your goals and sticking to your values.

THE BOTTOM LINE? YOU NOW HAVE PERMISSION TO STOP BEATING YOURSELF UP. SELF-COMPASSION ALLOWS YOU TO PERFORM BETTER AND COPE MORE EFFECTIVELY IN STRESSFUL SITUATIONS/MOMENTS THAT CHALLENGE YOU.

INNER COACH

Self-compassion is a pathway to mental toughness. The following exercises can get you thinking **the mentally tough way. The goal is to tap into your strongest and best inner coach!**

CHALLENGING MOMENTS

First, think about a time when a close friend felt really bad about him or herself and was really struggling. (For example, they missed the game winning shot, let the goal in and lost the game, made a bad play, struck out to end the game, forgot their lines in the scene, bombed a test, etc.) How could you have responded to your friend? What could you say to help them? Note the tone you use as well.

Now think about that same situation and put yourself in your friend's shoes. So you missed the game winning shot, let the goal in and lost the game, made the bad play, struck out, forgot your lines, bombed the test, etc. How do you typically respond to yourself in these situations? Write down what you typically do, what you say, and note the tone in which you talk to yourself.

Did you notice a difference? If so, ask yourself Why?" What factors or fears come into play that lead you to treat yourself and others so differently? Please write down how you think things might change if you responded to yourself in the same way you typically respond to a close friend. Why not try treating yourself like a good friend and see what happens?

COMPASSIONATE THINKING

This exercise was adapted from Paul Gilbert, author of *The Compassionate Mind*. Compassionate thinking invites us to think in a balanced way rather than thinking in an angry, anxious, frustrated way which may impact performance or our ability to pay attention to what matters most in a given moment. Think about a time in your performance that you find particularly challenging where your emotions (anger, anxiety, fear, frustration) take control of your thoughts.

Examples: "I'm not good enough." "I'm a loser." "This sucks."

The key is to be mindful of your thoughts and to stand back and observe them with the intention of trying to find the compassionate and balanced approach.

Write about a time in your performance where you are particularly self-critical (missed shot, benched by coach, turned the ball over, double-faulted, missed the training time, struck out, forgot your lines in a play, etc.) What would the <u>critical inner coach</u> in you say to yourself in that moment?

What is the emotional tone of the voice?

Is this thinking helpful to me?

Would I teach a child or friend to think this way?

If not, what would I encourage them to think in this moment?

How might I think in this moment when I am my best, most compassionate self?

"PERHAPS WE SHOULD LOVE OURSELVES SO FIERCELY THAT WHEN OTHERS SEE US THEY KNOW EXACTLY HOW IT'S DONE."

-RUDY FRANCISCO

MY MANTRA

me!

BUILDING YOUR COMPASSIONATE MANTRA*

Your mantra will be a phrase that you can turn to when you are being self-critical. By preparing for the moment ahead of time, you can set yourself up to more quickly get back in the game or the moment. First, think about identifying your most difficult moment in performance. Then, what did you most need to hear in that moment? If you have a hard time, consider thinking about what your favorite coach, friend, family member, or mentor would say to you in that moment. Make sure you note the emotional tone as well.

Examples: "I'll be okay, win or lose." "This is hard. Everyone has hard times." "Champions feel like this too." "I got this!" "No big deal, keep going!" "This is the way champions feel." "It's okay to feel this."

What is a difficult moment you face in your sport or performance (e.g., When I get scored on, after a turnover, sitting on the bench, when I get passed on the track, forgetting my lines on stage, hitting a wrong note in a concert, etc.)?

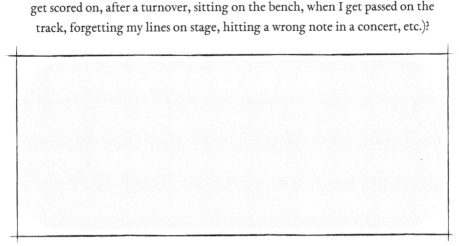

Now, what is your mantra? What do you most need to hear in that moment? Write it nice and big on the page to the left.

*This exercise is adapted from the MMTS protocol (*Mindfulness Meditation Training for Sport*) and a *Mindfulness and Performance* class at Boston University. See references for Amy Baltzell on page 286 to learn more.

"WHAT DO YOU DO WITH A MISTAKE: RECOGNIZE IT, ADMIT IT, LEARN FROM IT, FORGET IT."

— DEAN SMITH

BEING SELFLESS

Self-compassion might be the most selfless mental skill of them all. You don't rely on other people to pick you up in the face of failure or difficult times. After the missed shot, the bad pass, referee call against you, the disappointing test grade, etc., your teammates/coaches/friends don't need to pick you up. Your compassionate self gives you the courage to keep your head in the game and focused on the next play or the next action that you are in control of to get you closer to your goals and values.

How do YOU think being more self-compassionate will help your team?

How can you help remind your teammates of this strength and courage?

PRACTICING YOUR INNER COMPASSIONATE COACH

Use your compassionate thinking, mantra, or other wisdom you have gained to respond to each of the following prompts. Respond with a counter-argument - a new response to the event! Consider again the three components of self-compassion that may help you tap into that inner compassionate coach.

▸ I must criticize myself as a form of motivation.

_____

▸ I aim to be the best, better than everyone else! And, being not as good as others leaves me with a feeling of inadequacy.

_____

▸ Social comparisons and competitions happen often in my life.

_____

▸ I judge myself (particularly when facing failure or mistakes).

_____

▸ I become defensive when receiving criticism from a peer, coach, or teacher.

_____

▶ I fear failure.

▶ I avoid uncomfortable situations or feelings.

▶ I base my self-worth on performance results.

▶ I have felt embarrassed about a performance (test, play, concert, game, match, etc.) and felt alone in the experience.

▶ I feel guilty when I don't perform up to my potential.

▶ I feel angry when I miss the "easy" bucket, shot, goal, and have difficulty bouncing back or moving on quickly to the "next play."

▶ I blame myself after losses in competition.

COMPASSION FOR OTHERS

The Latin origin of the word compassion is "to suffer with." Compassion is an essential resource for thriving. When you make someone else laugh, smile, or feel good, or even when you give someone else a gift, it makes you feel good too. Showing others compassion and kindness can be as or more rewarding than receiving it. Researchers have confirmed that acting more compassionately is a behavior that can be learned. This is like a muscle where the more you flex it, the easier it becomes to use naturally. Practicing compassion helps you stay attuned to the emotions of others (and yourself) which, as an athlete, is a way to connect with your teammates and get the most out of yourself and your team.

"ALWAYS KEEP AN OPEN MIND AND A COMPASSIONATE HEART."

–PHIL JACKSON

Positivity and kindness feed off of each other, especially within a team environment. What better place to practice growing this core muscle than with your team.

In this exercise, think of four random acts of kindness to do for anyone related to your team. It could be a teammate, coach, manager, or someone that helps mow your fields or hand out your uniforms. Be creative and thoughtful in coming up with these actions. Look around you and think about what others might most need.

1.

2.

3.

4.

CHALK TALK
SPOT
DON'T FORGET TO S.T.O.P.
(THE BREATH RESET)
THROUGHOUT YOUR DAY!
P. 160

"IF YOU WANT
OTHERS TO BE HAPPY,
PRACTICE
COMPASSION. IF YOU
WANT TO BE HAPPY,
PRACTICE
COMPASSION."

— THE DALAI LAMA, XIV

KINDNESS
COUNTS

Now, let's suppose each of the four people that you reached out to repeat four acts of kindness the next day for four new people. Then those four people carry out acts of kindness for another four people the next day.

Here is what it would look like for the number of people touched by kindness each day

Kindness Counter	
	1 (This starts with YOU!)
Day 1	4
Day 2	16
Day 3	64
Day 4	256
Day 5	1,024
Day 6	4,096
Day 7	16,384

At the end of one week 16,384 people would have been touched by kindness. Now, consider doing that activity again for four people unrelated to your team and sport.

Focus on compassion for yourself and others, every day.

CHALK
TALK SPOT
SET A SPECIFIC DAY TO CARRY OUT YOUR ACTS OF KINDNESS FROM PAGE 197

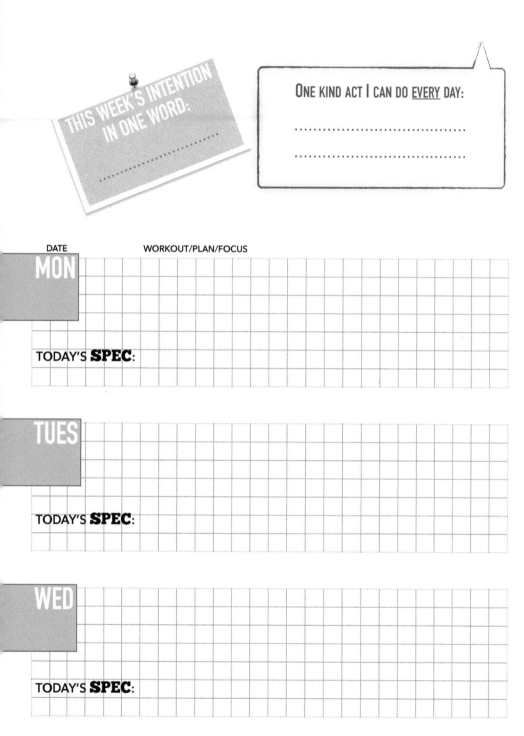

Reminder: Your daily **SPEC** is a small positive, enjoyable, and/or cool thing from your day!

200

DATE

THU

TODAY'S **SPEC**:

FRI

TODAY'S **SPEC**:

SAT

TODAY'S **SPEC**:

SUN

TODAY'S **SPEC**:

5 GRATITUDES FROM THE WEEK:

ZOOMING IN

| Creativity | Curiousity | Judgement | Perspective | Bravery | Perseverance |

| Zest | Honesty | Social Intelligence | Kindness | Love | Leadership |

WHAT WENT WELL this week in performance (or practice/training, if applicable)?

ON YOUR STRENGTHS...

Fairness	Teamwork	Forgiveness	Love of Learning	Gratitude	Spirituality

Self-Regulation	Humility	Appreciation of Beauty	Prudence	Hope	Humor

After reflecting on what went well, circle at least **three strengths you used** this week in practice, competition, or otherwise and give examples of each. Consider also your **signature strengths** and make sure you are practicing using those daily!

My signature strengths:
- ☑
- ☑
- ☑
- ☑
- ☑

TIME FOR T.W.C.

What is this week's challenge or something that did not go well? If it is something you can control and improve upon, make a plan for the coming week. If it is not something you can control, then consider writing it here and then turning the page as a symbolic gesture of letting it go.

CHECK IN...HOW ARE YOU DOING BALANCING YOUR PLATE <u>DAILY?</u>

Refer to page 30 if you need a refresher

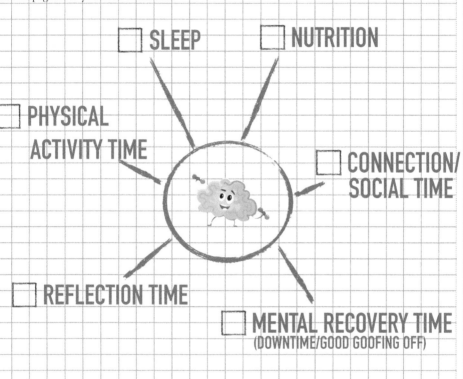

☐ SLEEP   ☐ NUTRITION

☐ PHYSICAL ACTIVITY TIME

☐ CONNECTION/ SOCIAL TIME

☐ REFLECTION TIME

☐ MENTAL RECOVERY TIME
(DOWNTIME/GOOD GOOFING OFF)

What steps will you take to make sure each of these essential elements are part of your upcoming week?

HUDDLE 8

RESILIENCE

"I REALLY THINK A CHAMPION IS DEFINED NOT BY THEIR WINS, BUT BY HOW THEY CAN RECOVER WHEN THEY FALL."

-SERENA WILLIAMS

HUDDLE 8
RESILIENCE

IN THIS HUDDLE:

▷ How do I build stress resilience?

▷ How should I handle pre-competition butterflies?

▷ What does hope have to do with anything?

▷ How can I practice finding the good and using humor to build my resilience?

Resilience is like your core muscles. Similar to how you need your core muscles to balance and have strength in all you do, building your resilience muscle as an athlete is vital to success. There are a few different ways to build your resilience.

You have four major core muscle groups —Rectus Abdominus (your abs), Obliques (on your sides allowing your trunk to twist), Transverse Abdomens (underneath obliques providing stability and protection), and Quadratus Lumborum (back muscle). Like your four major core muscles, you have four core *mental* muscles you can focus on to build resilience—**Perspective, Finding the Awesome, Hope, & Humor.**

I. PERSPECTIVE

Let's face it. Stress is inevitable. Rather than trying to avoid stress or push it away, you can take a different perspective —you can build stress resilience and view stress as your friend rather than your enemy. Health psychologist Kelly McGonigal has done research around stress resilience (watch her Ted Talk!). What she reveals is that the science shows that changing how you *think* about stress can actually make you healthier. So, you need to change your attitude about stress. When you change your thinking about stress, you can change the way your body responds to it.

"IF YOU CHANGE THE
WAY YOU LOOK AT
THINGS, THE THINGS
YOU LOOK AT
CHANGE."

-WAYNE DYER

LET THEM FLY

When you feel stress, you may feel your heart rate increase or you may start to sweat. Sometimes your breath pattern changes. Often people experience those feelings and sensations and think they are anxious or think it means they are not coping well. Studies show, however, that if you change the way you think about stress, and instead understand it as a way that your body is preparing you to meet a challenge, your performance improves. In other words, pre-competition or pre-performance when you feel those nerves or stress, tell yourself "bring it on!" You can thank your body for preparing you to meet the challenge. If you feel butterflies, **let them fly!**

The stress response and emotions such as fear and anxiety have evolved over time to help protect the human species. If you met up with a hungry lion on a path, you wouldn't have to think of what to do— the fight or flight response would kick in and you'd run. This negativity bias is part of our DNA. Walking into a class before a test, it is much easier to complain about your sleep or workload or fear about failing the test than it is to comment on the beautiful weather for the day or that you just had a nice breakfast with your friends. So, while negativity is easier, positivity and finding the good is not only possible but it will lead you to a full and flourishing life and set you up for greater success.

CHALK
TALK SPOT
CHALLENGE YOURSELF: WHAT
ARE YOU DOING TO MAKE
SOMEONE ELSE'S DAY
BETTER TODAY?

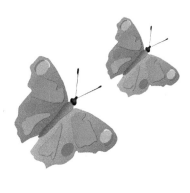

> ## "IT'S NOT WHAT YOU LOOK AT THAT MATTERS, IT'S WHAT YOU SEE."
>
> –HENRY DAVID THOREAU

How does your body respond to stress?

How do you usually feel during this stress response?

What perspective can you take on these feelings and on stress?

11. FIND THE AWESOME

One thing that research has shown can combat our negativity bias is gratitude. We explored gratitude in Huddle 4, but it's so important that it is worth coming back to.

In 2008, Neil Pasricha launched a blog 1000awesomethings.com, where he wrote an awesome thing for 1000 straight days from 2008 to 2012. Here are some examples:

Sleeping in new bed sheets;
Finding money you didn't even know you lost;
Sneezing three or more times in a row;
Sweatpants;
A really cold glass of water on a really hot day;
Snow days;
The sound of scissors cutting through construction paper;
Hitting a bunch of green lights in a row;
Roasting the perfect marshmallow;
High fiving babies;
The Five Second Rule;
When you get the milk to cereal ratio just right;
The smell of freshly cut grass;
Finding the TV remote after looking forever;
Letting go of the gas pump at just the right moment;
Fixing your wedgie when no one's looking;
When batteries are included;
The Kids Table;
Finally getting the popcorn seed out of your teeth;
The last day of school;
Sneaking cheap candy into the movie theater;
The other side of the pillow;
The first scoop out of a jar of peanut butter;
When cashiers open up new lanes at the grocery store.

Now it's your turn, come up with your own list of awesomeness and continue to add to it.

My super big ongoing list of awesomeness:

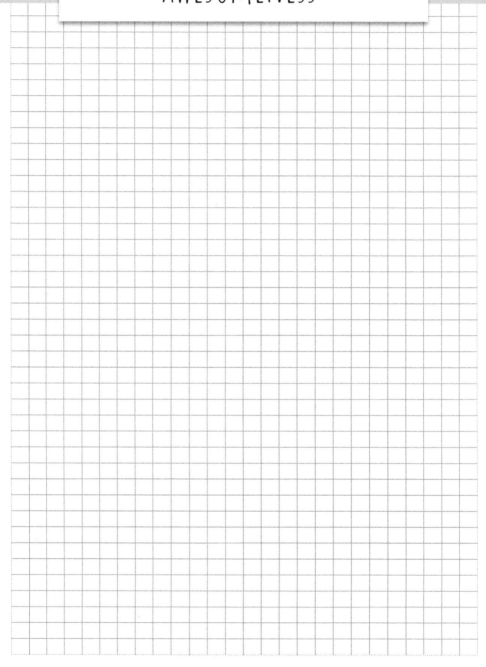

AWESOMENESS CONTINUED...

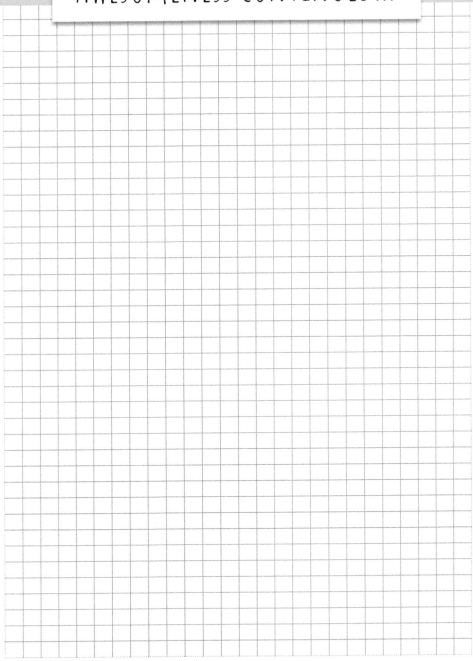

"OPTIMISM IS THE FAITH THAT LEADS TO ACHIEVEMENT. NOTHING CAN BE DONE WITHOUT HOPE AND CONFIDENCE."

-HELEN KELLER

III. HOPE

Hope and optimism both build your resilience. Hope is a special kind of optimism. It is not just seeing that things will get better, but knowing you can do something about it. Hope is also one of the primary components to what author and researcher Angela Duckworth calls *grit*. In her book, *Grit*, she shares the recipe for teaching yourself hope:

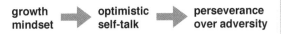

growth mindset ➡ **optimistic self-talk** ➡ **perseverance over adversity**

Duckworth says, "A growth mindset leads to optimistic ways of explaining adversity, and that, in turn, leads to perseverance and seeking out new challenges that will ultimately make you even stronger." (p. 192)

Building this muscle is going to help you in and outside of your team. Optimism is positively correlated with high levels of self-esteem, positive mood, happiness, life satisfaction, more resilience to stressful or negative events, prevention of illnesses, and recovery from illnesses, injuries, surgeries, and major life-events.

For teams, optimism generates positive emotions about the future and is important to every team member's well-being. Hope takes it one step further and is with you in the highs and lows of your season in a way that pushes you to persevere when things get hard. You reach for your goals because *you can*.

A study by Martin Seligman (a researcher, professor and author) was done with elite swimmers to test how they perform under pressure and after setbacks. Each swimmer took a test that measured how they respond to positive and negative events. Then at practice, they were asked to swim their best and as fast as possible. Afterwards, their coaches gave them a time that was slower than their actual time. Swimmers had some time (half an hour) to think about their performance and then were asked to swim the same race again. There was a clear difference between how the optimists and the pessimists performed on the second race, with the optimists actually racing the same or *faster* than in the first race and the pessimists racing *slower* than their first race. The pessimists spent their rest time annoyed and bummed about their disappointing time. Alternatively, the optimists were focused on learning and stretching their abilities, <u>and they did.</u>

Source: Martin Seligman, *Learned Optimism* (2006)

"CHOOSE TO BE OPTIMISTIC, IT FEELS BETTER."

–DALAI LAMA XIV

CHOOSE
OPTIMISM

Optimism can be learned. We can develop optimism through modeling (searching out and learning from someone who is already optimistic and taking note of how they handle situations), awareness (becoming more aware of our own thinking – more on that back in Huddle 6), and self-talk (also discussed in Huddle 2).

Here are some common ways athletes might react in a pessimistic versus optimistic way.

PESSIMISTIC	OPTIMISTIC
I cost us the game."	I played my hardest."
I'm awful." or Everyone is better than me."	This was challenging competition."
Bad luck will just keep following me."	I hope for the best and I'm ready to take on anything that comes my way."
I'm always on the weakest team."	I have an opportunity to regularly face the best competition and help my team improve."
There is no end in sight to our losing streak."	We'll learn from this loss and trust in the process."
We always lose to that team—we just can't compete with them."	We are excited by the challenge and it doesn't matter what happened in the past, this is a new game we will prepare for."
They are bigger, stronger, and faster than us."	We'll play to our strengths."
I'm in a slump."	My next opportunity could be the start of a new streak."

Practice creating optimistic self-talk statements after the following possible events. Use the extra spaces to add your own examples most relevant to you and in your sport.

EVENT	EXPLAINING THE EVENT USING OPTIMISTIC SELF-TALK
I get passed in the middle of the race.	
I missed the potential game winning shot (or penalty kick, etc.)	
My team has a losing record.	
My race time was not my best.	
My coach is very hard on me.	

Name two or three people in your life who you believe are optimists. Why do you consider them to be optimists?

Surround yourself with these people and let their optimism rub off on you!

What is the "glass is half full" approach to the rest of your season or year?

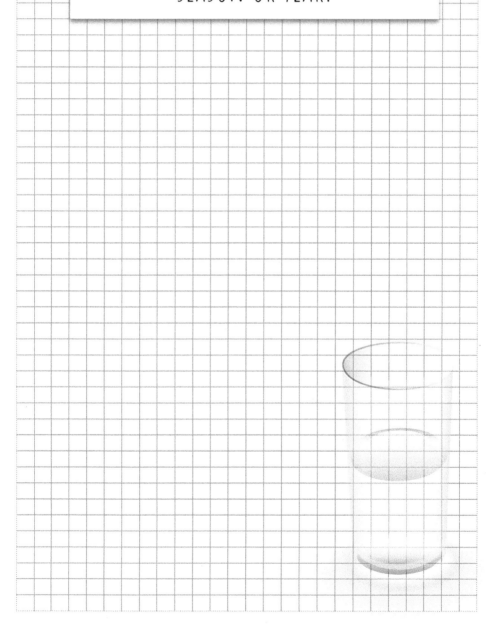

"YOU HAVE CHOICE, YOU ARE MASTER OF YOUR ATTITUDE, CHOOSE THE POSITIVE, THE CONSTRUCTIVE. OPTIMISM IS A FAITH THAT LEADS TO SUCCESS."

-BRUCE LEE

IV. HUMOR

Developing your humor muscle is much more than just telling jokes or laughing. The ability to laugh at yourself is actually something you can learn and practice over time (like perspective and all of the other muscles we have talked about).

Research shows that the use of humor helps relieve feelings of stress and anxiety. It can help you cope with difficult situations, bounce back quickly, and consequently build your resilience. Beyond the benefits to yourself, humor can bring you closer to your teammates as well as other people in your life. When you can laugh at yourself or see your own faults, the people around you will be more likely to let up on themselves. Humor helps you maintain perspective. No one is meant to be perfect.

What is FUN about your sport? What makes you smile?

FUNNY THINGS
HAPPENED TODAY

Humor can both help you cope with negative experiences as well more deeply appreciate the positive ones. As a twist on writing a daily "good thing," consider writing a *funny thing* from your day!

THREE THINGS THAT MADE ME LAUGH OR SMILE TODAY

1

2

3

CHALK
TALK SPOT
WHILE HUMOR HAS ITS BENEFITS, IT SHOULD NEVER COME AT THE EXPENSE OF SOMEONE ELSE. THAT MEANS YOU NEED TO FIND ALTERNATIVES TO GOSSIPING ABOUT AND WITH YOUR TEAMMATES AND SARCASTIC HUMOR (POKING FUN AT OTHERS). THIS IS PART OF BEING A LEADER.

Who and what makes you laugh?

What are some of your limitations? What are some things about yourself you can laugh about?

"WHEN YOU HAVE
FUN, IT CHANGES ALL
THE PRESSURE INTO
PLEASURE."

–KEN GRIFFEY SR. & JR.

THIS WEEK'S INTENTION IN ONE WORD:

....

PERSON WHO MAKES ME HAPPY:

....

....

DATE	WORKOUT/PLAN/FOCUS
MON	

TODAY'S **SPEC**:

TUES	

TODAY'S **SPEC**:

WED	

TODAY'S **SPEC**:

Reminder: Your daily **SPEC** is a small positive, enjoyable, and/or cool thing from your day!

THU

TODAY'S **SPEC**:

FRI

TODAY'S **SPEC**:

SAT

TODAY'S **SPEC**:

SUN

TODAY'S **SPEC**:

5 GRATITUDES FROM THE WEEK:

ZOOMING IN

Creativity	Curiousity	Judgement	Perspective	Bravery	Perseverance
Zest	Honesty	Social Intelligence	Kindness	Love	Leadership

WHAT WENT WELL this week in performance (or practice/training, if applicable)?

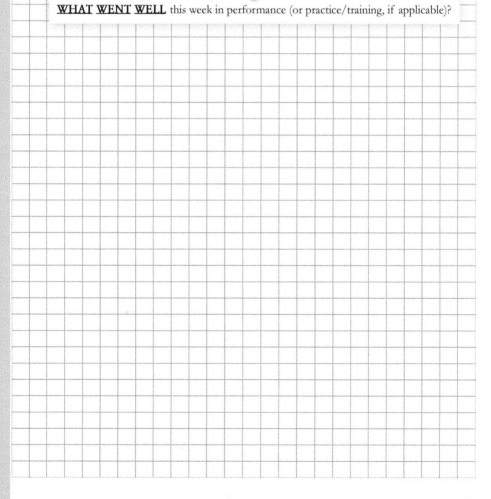

ON YOUR STRENGTHS...

Fairness	Teamwork	Forgiveness	Love of Learning	Gratitude	Spirituality
Self-Regulation	Humility	Appreciation of Beauty	Prudence	Hope	Humor

After reflecting on what went well, circle at least **three strengths you used** this week in practice, competition, or otherwise and give examples of each. Consider also your **signature strengths** and make sure you are practicing using those daily!

My signature strengths:

☑

☑

☑

☑

☑

TIME FOR T.W.C.

What is **this** **week's** **c**hallenge or something that did not go well? If it is something you can control and improve upon, make a plan for the coming week. If it is not something you can control, then consider writing it here and then turning the page as a symbolic gesture of letting it go.

CHECK IN...HOW ARE YOU DOING BALANCING YOUR PLATE DAILY?

Refer to page 30 if you need a refresher

☐ SLEEP   ☐ NUTRITION

☐ PHYSICAL ACTIVITY TIME

☐ CONNECTION/ SOCIAL TIME

☐ REFLECTION TIME

☐ MENTAL RECOVERY TIME
(DOWNTIME/GOOD GOOFING OFF)

What steps will you take to make sure each of these essential elements are part of your upcoming week?

HUDDLE 9

THE SWEET SPOT

"A TROPHY CARRIES DUST. MEMORIES LAST FOREVER."

-MARY LOU RETTON

HUDDLE 9
THE SWEET SPOT

This huddle is intended for you to reflect on the *sweet spot* - a place where you feel good and do good. Feeling good is not about the event, the situation, the score, the coach's decisions, the weather, the sore muscles, the failures, or the setbacks. With everything that happens, you have a choice. You can develop that space between stimulus (the event) and how you choose to respond. You can find the good, seek connections, do good for others, persevere, live by your values, be an optimist, hope and DO what it takes to make it better or reach for your goals. That's what leaders do.

Let's reflect a bit on your role(s), your strengths, and what you've learned throughout the journey thus far.

> "THE ROAD TO SUCCESS IS ALWAYS UNDER CONSTRUCTION."

–LILY TOMLIN

As we have discussed, on the road to feeling good and thriving, you must learn to shift focus from yourself to others. As you do good for others, you improve your own life as well. Ultimately, this is a path to being a real leader.

How have you contributed to the greater good of your community and/or team this season?

How have you used each of your signature character strengths in your sport or performance domain?

How have you approached the season with a
growth mindset and with an attitude of *thinking*
confidently?

What have you found works for you as a go-to
thought (if any) to say to yourself in high
pressure moments?

How have you made mindfulness (or simply
being present") a daily habit and
incorporated it in your training?

How can you change your perspective on
nerves and stress?

What are your go-to inspirational values that you stand by
no matter what the outcome or situation?

What are 4 things you are grateful for, big or small, with
respect to your sport?

"IT IS OUR CHOICES THAT SHOW WHAT WE TRULY ARE, FAR MORE THAN OUR ABILITIES."

-J.K. ROWLING

CHOICES

You have real choices in how you perceive events that happen and how you act. Here are some choices I hope for you:

CHOOSE BRAVE OVER PERFECT.

CHOOSE JOY OVER FEAR.

CHOOSE RESPONDING OVER REACTING.

CHOOSE COMPASSION OVER CRITICISM (OF SELF AND OTHERS).

CHOOSE POSITIVE OVER NEGATIVE.

CHOOSE OPTIMISM OVER PESSIMISM.

CHOOSE PROCESS OVER OUTCOME.

CHOOSE TO BE YOU OVER COMPARE.

CHOOSE "I GET TO" OVER "I HAVE TO."

CHOOSE ACCEPTANCE OVER JUDGEMENT.

"WE RISE BY LIFTING OTHERS."
-ROBERT ANGERSOLL

A final reflection: Joy is something available to you at any moment. Like confidence, you do not need to wait for it to come to you. You don't need to win a championship or a game to feel joy. Rather, you can find the satisfaction and joy in every situation. You will not be able to control everything that happens to you, but you can control your attitude about it and how you let it impact your life.

Yes, compete hard. Remember, compete means you **strive together.**

That means working towards a common goal without forgetting how important the "together" part is. In the first chapter we talked about how your attitude is contagious. Being a leader (in your school and community, on your team, and at your job) can actually be about you doing small things to build the mental muscles that increase your overall well-being as well as that of others.

You don't need to wait to get into the "best" college, get the perfect job, make a certain amount of money, or be voted captain to thrive and lead. Research study after research study show us that those external rewards do not necessarily contribute to greater well-being or better performance.

You don't need to let others control how you think or feel about anything. Your mind is your own.

> ## "I WILL NOT LET ANYONE WALK THROUGH MY MIND WITH THEIR DIRTY FEET."
>
> ### -GANDHI

Positivity and feeling good is not about being fearless, always happy, and believing life is hunky-dory all the time. It's about confronting fear (or anxiety or worry) and still doing your thing in spite of that. It's about acknowledging unwanted feelings or emotions and rather than trying to push them away, believing that you can rise above them, and putting your attention on the good or the action you most need to do in that moment. It's about creating your own path to joy and lasting happiness, understanding that it often goes straight through, not away from, challenges and adversity. It's developing mental toughness by building all of the mental muscles we have talked about (mindset, vision, gratitude, mindfulness, compassion, resilience, etc.). It's using your unique strengths, every day, to become the best version of YOU. It's knowing you have a choice in how you perceive your entire world. It is like giving yourself special lenses you get to wear so that the bumpy, windy, up and down journey you are on is just a little bit clearer, healthier, and more enjoyable.

Keep pounding the rock! Challenge yourself fiercely, put forward so much effort, and practice a bit outside of your comfort zone so that you can't possibly be perfect. Instead, **you will be unstoppable**. With that, I leave you with my definition of unstoppable:

UNSTOPPABLE /ADJ/:
THRIVING BY LEANING INTO CHALLENGES AND/OR SETBACKS WITH RELENTLESS EFFORT AND CHARACTER

Where you are
UNSTOPPABLE!

THE SWEET SPOT
WHERE YOU ARE AT YOUR BEST. DOING GOOD FOR YOURSELF AND THOSE AROUND YOU.

6 MENTAL MUSCLES

MINDSET (growth mindset, failure, confidence, self-talk, deliberate practice)

VISION (values, goal setting)

GRATITUDE (gratitude, savoring)

MINDFULNESS & ATTENTION (mindfulness, attention, meditation, flow)

COMPASSION (self-compassion, compassion, kindness)

RESILIENCE (perspective, finding the awesome, hope, humor)

3 LEADERSHIP ROLES

DESIGNATED LEADER
PEER LEADER
SELF LEADER

YOUR STRENGTHS

YOUR PERSONALITY, STRENGTHS, AND STYLE

It's on YOU!

Fill in the chart below.

THE SWEET SPOT
WHERE YOU ARE AT YOUR BEST. DOING GOOD FOR YOURSELF AND THOSE AROUND YOU.

MENTAL MUSCLES I HAVE GROWN & WILL CONTINUE TO PRACTICE:

MY LEADERSHIP ROLES & RESPONSIBILITIES I AM COMMITTED TO:

MY STRENGTHS:

SOMETHING I LOVE ABOUT ME:

....

....

DATE   WORKOUT/PLAN/FOCUS

MON

TODAY'S **SPEC**:

TUES

TODAY'S **SPEC**:

WED

TODAY'S **SPEC**:

Reminder: Your daily **SPEC** is a small positive, enjoyable, and/or cool thing from your day!

THU

TODAY'S **SPEC**:

FRI

TODAY'S **SPEC**:

SAT

TODAY'S **SPEC**:

SUN

TODAY'S **SPEC**:

5 GRATITUDES FROM THE WEEK:

ZOOMING IN

Creativity

Curiousity

Judgement

Perspective

Bravery

Perseverance

Zest

Honesty

Social Intelligence

Kindness

Love

Leadership

WHAT WENT WELL this week in performance (or practice/training, if applicable)?

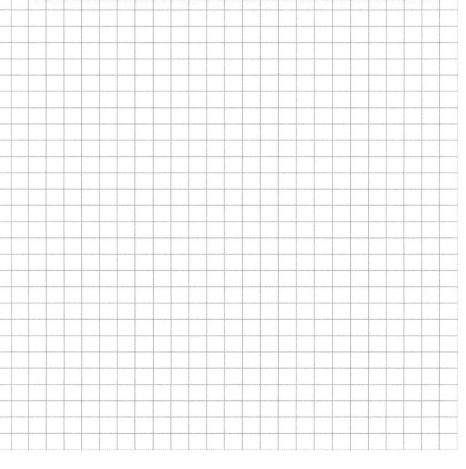

ON YOUR STRENGTHS...

| Fairness | Teamwork | Forgiveness | Love of Learning | Gratitude | Spirituality |

| Self-Regulation | Humility | Appreciation of Beauty | Prudence | Hope | Humor |

After reflecting on what went well, circle at least **three strengths you used** this week in practice, competition, or otherwise and give examples of each. Consider also your **signature strengths** and make sure you are practicing using those daily!

My signature strengths:

☑

☑

☑

☑

☑

TIME FOR T.W.C.

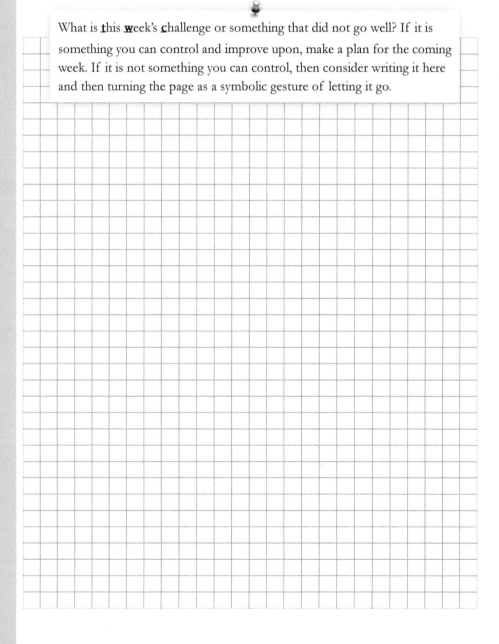

What is this week's challenge or something that did not go well? If it is something you can control and improve upon, make a plan for the coming week. If it is not something you can control, then consider writing it here and then turning the page as a symbolic gesture of letting it go.

CHECK IN... HOW ARE YOU DOING BALANCING YOUR PLATE DAILY?

Refer to page 30 if you need a refresher

☐ SLEEP   ☐ NUTRITION

☐ PHYSICAL ACTIVITY TIME

☐ CONNECTION/ SOCIAL TIME

☐ REFLECTION TIME

☐ MENTAL RECOVERY TIME
(DOWNTIME/GOOD GOOFING OFF)

What steps will you take to make sure each of these essential elements are part of your upcoming week?

APPENDICES

APPENDIX A:
HUDDLE 10 —OFFSEASON REFLECTION

The offseason is a time to rest, recover, and reflect.

For those athletes or teams where it is applicable, you may consider this Appendix like another Huddle. Save it until after your season or when the moment feels right to reflect on your goals and make new ones. Take time to really savor moments and learn from challenges. Ultimately, as time goes on you may find that you remember the relationships formed throughout the journey much more than scores or records.

Use the space below to jot down the names of your teammates, coaches, and supporters who had an impact on you.

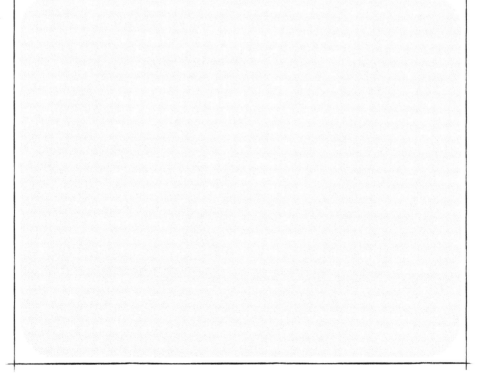

"IF YOU LAUGH, YOU THINK, AND YOU CRY, THAT'S A FULL DAY. YOU DO THAT SEVEN DAYS A WEEK, YOU'RE GOING TO HAVE SOMETHING SPECIAL."

-JIM VALVANO

REFLECT

SUCCESSES:

CHALLENGES I FACED:

THINGS I DID I'D LIKE TO DO AGAIN NEXT YEAR:

THINGS I WOULD LIKE TO DO DIFFERENTLY NEXT YEAR:

MY PERFORMANCE GOAL(S) I MADE THIS SEASON (PAGE 114):

HOW DID IT GO?

MY WELLNESS GOAL(S) I MADE THIS SEASON (PAGE 124):

HOW DID IT GO?

LEADERSHIP ROLES I FILLED
THIS SEASON AND HOW
(HUDDLE 1):

MENTAL MUSCLES THAT
GREW THE BIGGEST:

- ☐ GROWTH MINDSET
- ☐ CONFIDENCE
- ☐ GRATITUDE
  - ☐ SAVORING
- ☐ MINDFULNESS
- ☐ SELF-COMPASSION
- ☐ COMPASSION/KINDNESS
- ☐ RESILIENCE
  - ☐ STRESS PERSPECTIVE
  - ☐ FINDING THE AWESOME
  - ☐ HOPE
  - ☐ HUMOR

MENTAL MUSCLES THAT
STILL FEEL WEAK:

Remember to keep your muscles strong,
you need to practice continually the
mental toughness skills you learned here.
Make them a part of who you are, how
you think, and how you act daily!

CHARACTER STRENGTHS I
USED THE MOST THIS SEASON:

CHARACTER STRENGTHS I
SPOTTED IN MY TEAMMATES:

MY FAVORITE MOMENT FROM THE SEASON:

LOOK BACK AT THE LETTER YOU WROTE TO YOURSELF AT
THE START OF THE SEASON. READ IT. THEN USE THIS SPACE
TO REFLECT ON IT. WAS THERE ANYTHING YOU LEARNED
THAT YOU WOULD SAY TO YOURSELF NEXT TIME? ANYTHING
YOU MOST APPRECIATE ABOUT YOUR LETTER TO YOURSELF?

"KEEP YOUR HEAD UP, KEEP YOUR HEART STRONG."

-SHALANE FLANAGAN

HOW DID YOU DO AS A WHOLE BALANCING YOUR DAILY PLATE THIS SEASON?

☐ SLEEP   ☐ NUTRITION

☐ PHYSICAL ACTIVITY TIME

☐ CONNECTION/ SOCIAL TIME

☐ REFLECTION TIME

☐ MENTAL RECOVERY TIME
(DOWNTIME/GOOD GOOFING OFF)

WAYS I PRIORITIZED SLEEP:

ACTION PLAN TO CONTINUE TO PRIORITIZE IT:

WAYS I PRIORITIZED GOOD
NUTRITION:

ACTION PLAN TO CONTINUE TO
PRIORITIZE IT:

WAYS I FOUND CONNECTION &
SOCIAL TIME:

ACTION PLAN TO CONTINUE TO
HAVE SOCIAL TIME EACH DAY:

WAYS I FOUND MENTAL
RECOVERY TIME DAILY
(DOWNTIME OR GOOD GOOFING
OFF TIME):

ACTION PLAN TO CONTINUE TO
HAVE MENTAL RECOVERY TIME
DAILY:

WAYS I FOUND TIME TO
REFLECT DAILY:

ACTION PLAN TO CONTINUE TO
PRIORITIZE TIME, EVEN SMALL
AMOUNTS, OF REFLECTION
DAILY:

33 HABITS FOR FUELING PERFORMANCE (& FLOURISHING!)

Remember how important forming habits is. Practicing your sport once isn't enough to create excellence. That is obvious. But the same goes for building your leadership, strengths, and mental muscles we have talked about. Each of the huddles in this book has areas you can practice to grow your mental muscles and become *unstoppable* (and happier, more resilient, mentally stronger, etc.) The 33 habits below chosen with great thought and research to help you *fuel from within*. You have what it takes inside you. Now make it happen.

- [ ] BE KIND.
- [ ] SURROUND YOURSELF WITH PEOPLE WHO LIFT YOU UP.
- [ ] LIFT OTHERS UP.
- [ ] PRACTICE SELF-COMPASSION.
- [ ] FIND FLOW.
- [ ] BRING MINDFULNESS INTO YOUR EVERY DAY.
- [ ] MEDITATE.
- [ ] GET OUTSIDE.
- [ ] DREAM BIG.
- [ ] CHOOSE ALTERNATIVES TO GOSSIP.
- [ ] EXPRESS GRATITUDE.
- [ ] VIEW STRESS AS A CHALLENGE, NOT A THREAT.
- [ ] LET GO OF JUDGMENTS.
- [ ] BELIEVE.
- [ ] PRACTICE PURPOSEFULLY.
- [ ] BE RECEPTIVE TO FEEDBACK (FOCUS—FEEDBACK—FIX IT).
- [ ] SAY GOODBYE TO EXCUSES.
- [ ] VIEW MISTAKES/FAILURES AS OPPORTUNITIES TO GROW.
- [ ] EAT WELL.
- [ ] DRINK WATER.
- [ ] NOTICE AND SAVOR THE GOOD.
- [ ] FOCUS ON THE PROCESS, NOT THE OUTCOME.
- [ ] KEEP A HEALTHY SLEEP ROUTINE.
- [ ] REFLECT (DAILY) ON GOOD THINGS.
- [ ] FOCUS ON THE THINGS WITHIN YOUR CONTROL. LET GO OF WHAT YOU CAN'T.
- [ ] BE COMFORTABLE BEING UNCOMFORTABLE.
- [ ] CHOOSE OPTIMISM.
- [ ] STICK TO YOUR VALUES.
- [ ] CHOOSE TO BELIEVE HELPFUL THOUGHTS, NOT UNHELPFUL THOUGHTS.
- [ ] BRING YOUR STRENGTHS FORWARD EVERY DAY.
- [ ] PRACTICE VISUALIZATION.
- [ ] STAND TALL AND THINK CONFIDENTLY.
- [ ] CHOOSE TO BE UNSTOPPABLE OVER PERFECT.

CHECK OFF THE HABITS YOU ALREADY HAVE

"THINGS TURN OUT
BEST FOR THE PEOPLE
WHO MAKE THE
BEST OF THE WAY
THINGS TURN OUT."

–JOHN WOODEN

HEALTHY COPING STRATEGIES:

IT'S OKAY TO ACKNOWLEDGE THE INJURY STINKS AND FEEL SAD AND/OR FRUSTRATED ABOUT IT.

THEN, MOVE FORWARD & GET BUSY.......

MAINTAIN A POSITIVE ATTITUDE.

FIND WAYS TO "WORK OUT" EVEN IF JUST THROUGH MENTAL IMAGERY.

BE WITH YOUR TEAM, IF YOU CAN, DURING PRACTICES AND COMPETITIONS.

SEEK SUPPORT FROM YOUR TEAMMATES AND LET THEM KNOW WHAT YOU NEED.

FOCUS ON JOY OVER PAIN. (OPTIMISM, GRATITUDE, SAVORING GOOD MOMENTS, ETC.)

TAKE AN ACTIVE ROLE IN GETTING BETTER.

SEEK HELP FROM A COUNSELOR –THIS IS A SIGN OF STRENGTH.

PRACTICE PATIENCE.

"THE STRUGGLE ENDS WHEN THE GRATITUDE BEGINS." – NEALE DONALD WALSCH

APPENDIX F:
IDENTIFYING CHARACTER STRENGTHS
PAPER TEST

Looking at the list of strengths below, rate each one on a 1-10 basis (1 is "not at all like me" and 10 is "totally like me!"). Write your answer in the space after each.

Try to be <u>honest</u> and score them according to how you are, not how you'd like to be!

Creativity: Thinking of novel and productive ways to conceptualize and do things (not just artsy things!)

_____

Curiosity: Taking an interest in a wide variety of experiences; finding subjects and topics fascinating; exploring and discovering

_____

Judgment/Open-mindedness: Thinking things through and examining them from all sides; not jumping to conclusions; being able to change one's mind in light of evidence; weighing all evidence fairly

_____

Love of Learning: Mastering new skills, topics, and bodies of knowledge, whether on one's own or formally; obviously related to the strength of curiosity but goes beyond it to describe the tendency to add systematically to what one knows

_____

Wisdom: Being able to provide wise counsel to others; having ways of looking at the world that make sense to oneself and to other people

_____

Bravery: Not shrinking from threat, challenge, difficulty, or pain; speaking up for what is right even if there is opposition; acting on convictions even if unpopular; not limited to physical bravery

_____

Perseverance: Finishing what one starts; persisting in a course of action in spite of obstacles, not giving up

_____

Honesty: Speaking the truth; presenting oneself in a genuine way and acting sincerely; taking responsibility for your own feelings and actions

_____

Zest/Enthusiasm: Approaching life with excitement and energy; not doing things halfway or half-heartedly; feeling alive and activated

_____

Love: Valuing close relations with others, in particular those in which sharing and caring are reciprocated; being close to people

_____

Kindness: Doing favors and good deeds for others; helping them; taking care of them

_____

Social Intelligence: Being aware of the motives and feelings of other people and yourself; knowing what to do to fit into different social situations; knowing how to look after other people

_____

Teamwork: Working well as a member of a group or team; being loyal to the group _____

Fairness: Treating all people the same according to notions of fairness and justice; not letting personal feelings bias decisions about others; giving everyone a fair chance _____

Leadership: Encouraging a group to get things done while maintaining good relations within the group; organizing group activities and seeing that they happen _____

Forgiveness: Forgiving those who have done wrong; accepting the shortcoming of others; giving people a second chance; not being vengeful _____

Humility/Modesty: Letting your accomplishments speak for themselves; not regarding yourself as more special than others _____

Prudence/Cautious: Being careful about your choices; not taking undue risks; not saying or doing things that might later be regretted _____

Self-Control: Regulating what you feel and do; being disciplined; controlling your appetite and emotions _____

Appreciation of Beauty and Excellence: Appreciating beauty, excellence, and/or skilled performance in various domains of life _____

Gratitude: Being aware of and thankful for the good things that happen; taking them to express thanks _____

Hope: Expecting the best in the future and working to achieve it _____

Humor: Liking to laugh and tease; making other people smile/laugh; seeing the light side _____

Spirituality/Faith: Having coherent beliefs about a higher purpose, the meaning of life and the meaning of the universe _____

Now, identify your Signature Strengths by picking the strengths with your TOP 3-6 (ish) scores and asking yourself the following questions:

☑ Is this the real me?

☑ Do I enjoy using this strength?

☑ Does using this strength energize me?

Adapted from New Zealand Institute of Wellbeing & Resilience

My signature strengths:

☑ _____

☑ _____

☑ _____

☑ _____

☑ _____

☑ _____

285

REFERENCES AND RECOMMENDED READING

BOOKS:

Afremow, Jim. *The Champion's Mind: How Great Athletes Think, Train, and Thrive.* New York: Rodale Books, 2013.

Afremow, Jim. *The Champion's Comeback: How Great Athletes Recover, Reflect, and Re-Ignite.* New York: Rodale, 2016.

Anchor, Shawn. *The Happiness Advantage: The Seven Principles that Fuel Success and Performance at Work.* London, UK: Virgin Books, 2011

Baltzell, Amy. *Living in the sweet spot: preparing for performance in sport & life.* Morgantown, WV: Fitness Information Technology, 2011.

Baltzell, Amy, editor. *Mindfulness and Performance: Current Perspectives in Social and Behavior Sciences.* New York: Cambridge University Press, 2017.

Baltzell, Amy and Joshua Summers. *The Power of Mindfulness: Mindfulness Meditation Training in Sport (MMTS).* Springer International Publishing, 2017.

Carter, Christine. *Raising Happiness.* Ballantine Books, 2010.

Cope, Andy and Amy Bradley. *The Little Book of Emotional Intelligence.* London: John Murray Learning, 2016

Duckworth, Angela. *Grit: The Power of Passion and Perseverance.* New York: Simon & Schuster, 2016.

Duhigg, Charles. *The Power of Habit: Why We Do What We Do in Life and Business.* New York: Random House, 2012.

Doige, Norman. *The Brain That Changes Itself.* New York: Penguin Group, 2007

Dweck, Carol S. *Mindset: The New Psychology of Success.* New York: Ballantine Books, 2008.

Ericsson, K. Anders, and Robert Pool. *Peak: Secrets from the New Science of Expertise.* New York: Houghton Mifflin Harcourt, 2016.

Fabritius, Friederike, and Hans W. Hagemann. *The Leading Brain: Powerful Science-Based Strategies for Achieving Peak Performance.* New York: Penguin Random House, 2017

Fredrickson, Barbara. *Positivity: Top-Notch Research Reveals the Upward Spiral That Will Change Your Life.* Crown Publishers, 2009.

Gallwey, W. Timothy. *The Inner Game of Tennis: The Classic Guide to the Mental Side of Peak Performance.* New York: Random House Trade Paperbacks, 2008.

Goon, John and Shari Leach, editors. *Leadership Educator Notebook: A toolbox for Leadership Educators 5th edition.* Lander Wyoming, 2012.

Gordon, Jon. *The Power of Positive Leadership: How and Why Positive Leaders Transform Teams and Organizations and Change the World.* Hoboken, NJ: Wiley, 2017.

Jackson, Susan A., and Csíkszentmihályi Mihály. *Flow in Sports: The Keys to Optimal Experiences and Performances.* Champaign, IL: Human Kinetics, 1999.

Kornfield, Jack. *Meditation for Beginners.* Boulder CO: Sounds True, 2008.

Abrams, Douglas, Dalai Lama, and Desmond Tutu. *The Book of Joy: Lasting Happiness in a Changing World*. New York: Penguin Random House, 2016.

Mack, Gary, and David Casstevens. *Mind Gym: An Athletes Guide to Inner Excellence*. New York: McGraw-Hill, 2001.

Medina, John. *Brain Rules: 12 Principles for Surviving and Thriving at Work, Home, and School*. Seattle, WA: Pear Press, 2014.

Mumford, George. *The Mindful Athlete: Secrets to Pure Performance*. Berkeley, CA: Parallax Press, 2015.

Neff, Kristin. *Self-Compassion: The Proven Power of Being Kind to Yourself*. New York: Harper Collins, 2011

Niemiec, Ryan M. *Mindfulness and Character Strengths: A Practical Guide to Flourishing*. Boston: Hogrefe, 2013.

Oettingen, Gabriele. *Rethinking Positive Thinking: Inside the New Science of Motivation*. New York: Penguin Group, 2014.

Orlick, Terry. *In Pursuit of Excellence: How to Win in Sports and Life through Mental Training*. Champaign, IL: Human Kinetics, 2008.

Pasricha, Neil. *The Happiness Equation: Want Nothing + Do Anything = Have Everything*. New York: G.P. Putnam's Sons, 2016.

Seligman, Martin E. P. *Learned optimism*. New York: Vintage Books, 2006.

Seligman, Martin E. P. *Flourish: A Visionary New Understanding of Happiness and Well-Being*. New York: Simon & Schuster, 2012.

Selk, Jason. *10-Minute Toughness: The Mental Training Program for Winning Before the Game Begins*. New York: McGraw-Hill, 2009.

Stahl, Bob, and Elisha Goldstein. *A Mindfulness-Based Stress Reduction Workbook*. Oakland, CA: New Harbinger Publications, 2010.

Waters, Lea. *The Strength Switch: How the New Science of Strength-Based Parenting Helps Your Child and Your Teen Flourish*. New York: Penguin Random House, 2017.

Weinberg, R.S. & Gould, D. (2003). Foundations of sport and exercise psychology. (5th Edition). Champaign, IL: Human Kinetics.

Williams, Jean Marie, and Vikki Krane. *Applied Sport Psychology: Personal Growth to Peak Performance*. (7th Edition). New York: McGraw-Hill education, 2015.

ARTICLES:

American Academy of Sleep Medicine. (2013). Fatigue and sleep linked to Major League Baseball performance and career longevity. *ScienceDaily*. Retrieved November 16, 2017 from www.sciencedaily.com/releases/2013/05/130531105506.htm

Baltzell, A., Caraballo, N., Chipman, K., and Laura Hayden. (2014). A Qualitative Study of the Mindfulness Meditation Training for Sport: Division I Female Soccer Players' Experience. Journal of Clinical Sport Psychology, 8, 221-224.

Baltzell, A., LoVerme Akhtar, V. (2014). Mindfulness meditation training for sport (MMTS) intervention: Impact of MMTS with division I female athletes. The Journal of Happiness & Well-Being, 2(2), 160-173.

Gilbert, P. (2010). Training Our Minds in, with and for Compassion An Introduction to Concepts and Compassion-Focused Exercises, 1-82. Retrieved June 26, 2017, from http://wtm.thebreathproject.org/wp-content/uploads/2016/03/COMPASSION-HANDOUT.pdf

Hays, K.F. (2010). The Breathing Edge. Retrieved September 27, 2017, from https://www.psychologytoday.com/blog/the-edge-peak-performance-psychology/201001/the-breathing-edge-part-i

Kageyama, N. (2014). Self-Compassion: Does It Help or Hinder Performance? Retrieved June 27, 2017, from http://www.bulletproofmusician.com/self-compassion-does-it-help-or-hinder-performance/

Seligman, M. E., Steen, T. A., Park, N., & Peterson, C. (2005). Positive psychology progress: Empirical validation of interventions. American Psychologist, 60(5), 410.

Mosewich, A.D., Kowalski, K.C., Sabiston, C.M., Sedgwick, W.A., & Tracy, J.L. (2011). Self-compassion: A potential resource for young women athletes. Journal of Sport & Exercise Psychology, 103-123; PubMed

Mosewich, A. D., Crocker, P. R. E., Kowalski, K. & DeLongis, A. (2013). Applying self-compassion in sport: An intervention with women athletes. Journal of Sport & Exercise Psychology, 35, 514-524.

Neff, K. (2011). Why Self-Compassion Trumps Self-Esteem. Retrieved June 27, 2017, from https://greatergood.berkeley.edu/article/item/try_selfcompassion

Neff, K.D.,& Germer, G.K. (2013). A pilot study and randomized control trial of the Mindful Self-Compassion program. Journal of Clinical Psychology, 28-44. PubMed doi: 10.1002/jclp.21923

Reis, N. A., Kowalski, K. C., Ferguson, L. J., Sabiston, C. M., Sedgwick, W. A., & Crocker, P. R. E. (2015). Self-compassion and women athletes' responses to emotionally difficult sport situations: An evaluation of a brief induction. Psychology of Sport and Exercise, 16, 18-25.

Ryan, R.M., Deci, E.L. (2000). Self-Determination Theory and the Facilitation of Intrinsic Motivation. Social Development, and Well-Being. American Psychologist, 55, 68-78. doi: 10.1037110003-066X.55.1.68

WEBSITES:

1000 Awesome Things (http://1000awesomethings.com)

Authentic Happiness (http://www.authentichappiness.sas.upenn.edu)

Calm (www.calm.com)

The Character Lab (http://www.characterlab.org)

Greater Good Science Center at the University of California at Berkley (www.greatergood.berkeley.edu)

Happify (www.happify.com)

Headspace (www.headspace.com)

Mindset (www.mindsetonline.org)

New Zealand Institute for Wellbeing and Resilience (http://nziwr.co.nz/)

NOLS – The Leader in Wilderness Education (http://www.nols.edu)

Self-Compassion (www.self-compassion.org)

The Positivity Project (http://posproject.org)

Tiny Habits® (http://tinyhabits.com)

VIA Institute (www.viacharacter.org)

WOOP (www.woopmylife.org)

CONTRIBUTER WEBSITES:

tarynburnsyoga.com

the-mindful-way.com

For more resources including links to recommended TedTalks, websites, videos, and books, visit **www.lanisilversides.com**

Batch 526120BV00003B

526120BVX00003B	9781495821097	Machine Free Fitness: 150+ Exercises Th		
PERFECT	5.50X8.50	398	GLOSS	(30
526120BVX00004B	9780692157626	UNSTOPPABLE: A Mental Training Gu		
PERFECT	6.00X9.00	292	GLOSS	(20
526120BVX00005B	9780741468420	Transformed		
PERFECT	5.50X8.50	170	GLOSS	(50
526120BVX00006B	9781948400435	Whose Bad @$$ Kids are Those?: A Par		
PERFECT	4.37X7.00	70	GLOSS	(88

526120BV00003B/5

CTNQTY-SR:COLORSTD70

PERFECT

26120BVX00003B - 526120BVX00006B [4 : 188]

* 5 2 6 1 2 0 B V 0 0 0 0 3 B *

3OOK
TCO7019_SM

epartment	Operator's Name (Please print)
:inting	_____
inding	_____
utting	_____
hipping	_____
atch Location	_____

* 5 2 6 1 2 0 B V *

Promise Date: 07-SEP-18

inted at: Sun Sep 2 07:23:26 2018 on device bvhp06-50

....

MY FAVORITE POST–COMPETITION MEAL:

....

....

DATE   WORKOUT/PLAN/FOCUS

MON

TODAY'S **SPEC**:

TUES

TODAY'S **SPEC**:

WED

TODAY'S **SPEC**:

WORKOUT/PLAN/FOCUS

DATE

THU

TODAY'S **SPEC**:

FRI

TODAY'S **SPEC**:

SAT

TODAY'S **SPEC**:

SUN

TODAY'S **SPEC**:

5 GRATITUDES FROM THE WEEK:

APPENDIX C:
RECIPE SHEET FOR HABIT FORMATION

Following BJ Fogg's Tiny Habits® recipe (page 29), here is a recipe sheet you can use to help form new habits:

PROMPT: What is something you already do in your day?

After _____,

Ideas: wake up, flush a toilet, wash hands, step onto the field/court, turn on/off the shower, brush teeth, lock the door, etc.

NEW HABIT: What new habit would you like to start doing? Remember you can start small and add more later!

I will _____

CELEBRATE: Give yourself even a small reward to complete the habit formation loop (pg. 28).

and I will reward myself by _____

Ideas: clap, snap your fingers, say "YES!", give yourself a high-five, give yourself a pat on the back, sing, do a little dance, do a little shimmy with your shoulders, give a thumbs up, take a bow, smile, etc.

APPENDIX D: RECOVERY YOGA POSES REFERENCE SHEET

There are some yoga poses every athlete should have in their toolbox, especially when facing sore muscles from a tough workout. Combine these with the breathing you learned and you can help your muscles recover while increasing your mobility and flexibility as well. Visit the online Resource Training Room for more!

FORWARD BEND

EXHALE AS YOU FOLD DOWN, LETTING YOUR HEAD,/ NECK/SHOULDERS FEEL HEAVY. TRY TO GET YOUR BELLY TO TOUCH YOUR THIGHS. YOU MAY NEED A SLIGHT BEND IN YOUR KNEES TO DO THIS. THEN FOLLOW REGULAR DEEP BREATHING. ON AN EXHALE YOU CAN TRY FOLDING DEEPER.

CAT/COW

EXHALE DEEPLY AS YOU ARCH YOUR BACK LIKE AN ANGRY CAT. THEN INHALE AS YOU DROP YOUR CORE TOWARD THE FLOOR. THEN REPEAT A FEW TIMES.

THREAD THE NEEDLE

FROM ALL FOURS WITH KNEES SPREAD A LITTLE WIDER THAN SHOULDER WIDTH APART. INHALE AND BRING YOUR LEFT ARM UP OPENING UP YOUR CHEST EXTENDING TOWARD THE CEILING. ROTATE YOUR BODY DOWNWARD AND EXHALE BRINGING THE ARM DOWN AND THROUGH THE SPACE BETWEEN YOUR OPPOSITE ARM AND LEG RESTING YOUR SHOULDER ON THE GROUND. REPEAT FOR A FEW BREATHS ON EACH SIDE.

TREE POSE

MAKE SURE YOUR FOOT IS ABOVE YOUR KNEE ON YOUR INNER THIGH OR ON YOUR SHIN (NEVER ON YOUR KNEE). THIS IS A HIP OPENER. TRY TO KEEP YOUR BENT KNEE OUT AND OPEN.

Step 1

Step 2

SUPINE TWIST

LIE ON YOUR BACK WITH THE SOLES OF YOUR FEET ON THE GROUND OR MAT. KNEES TOGETHER. DROP YOUR LEGS TO ONE SIDE STACKING YOUR HIPS. BRING YOUR ARMS OUT TO A "T" AND LOOK OVER YOUR SHOULDER OPPOSITE THE DIRECTION THAT YOU HAVE YOUR LEGS. REPEAT ON THE OTHER SIDE.

DOWNWARD DOG

START ON ALL FOURS. BRING YOUR BELLY UP AND IN. PUSH YOUR HIPS TOWARD THE CEILING STAYING ON THE BALLS OF YOUR FEET. STAY SOFT THROUGH YOUR SHOULDERS AND ARMS REMEMBERING TO BREATHE. THERE MAY BE A SLIGHT BEND TO THE KNEES. KEEP YOUR SHOULDERS, BACK, NECK, AND ARMS ALL IN A STRAIGHT LINE. SPREAD YOUR FINGERS. RESUME YOUR DEEP BELLY BREATHING.

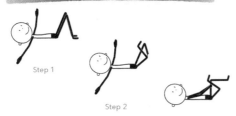

Step 1

Step 2

Step 3

FIGURE 4

LIE ON YOUR BACK AND PLANT YOUR FEET TO THE GROUND. CROSS YOUR RIGHT ANKLE OVER YOUR LEFT THIGH TO CREATE A FIGURE 4. YOU CAN TREAD YOUR HANDS THROUGH AND PULL YOUR LEFT HAMSTRING. KEEP BACK/NECK/HEAD ALL FLAT ON THE GROUND OR MAT. ON YOUR INHALE YOU CAN LET YOUR LEG GO FORWARD AND ON THE EXHALE YOU CAN BRING IT CLOSER TO YOU.

CHILD'S POSE

START ON ALL FOURS. SINK BACK ONTO YOUR HEALS. YOU MAY WANT TO SPREAD YOUR LEGS A LITTLE WIDER. GROUND YOUR FOREHEAD INTO THE MAT. KEEP A FLAT BACK. RESUME REGULAR DEEP BELLY BREATHING.

LEGS ON THE WALL

BRING YOUR BOTTOM AS CLOSE TO A WALL AS YOU CAN AND PUT YOUR FEET UP. OPEN YOUR ARMS TO THE SIDE. CLOSE YOUR EYES IF YOU ARE COMFORTABLE AND RESUME YOUR DEEP BELLY BREATHING.

LOW RUNNERS LUNGE

FROM DOWN DOG, STEP A FOOT UP TO YOUR HANDS AND DROP YOUR BACK KNEE AND UNTUCK YOUR TOES. BRING YOUR ARMS UP IN THE AIR ON AN INHALE. DO A COUPLE OF BREATHS AND ON THE INHALE TRY TO ELONGATE WITH YOUR ARMS.

APPENDIX E:
COPING WITH INJURIES REFERENCE SHEET

It can be extremely challenging for athletes to deal with injuries in or outside of their season. Optimal injury rehabilitation requires both physical and psychological components. When done well, injuries often heal faster, psychological adjustment is healthier, and higher levels of performance resume more quickly.

Discovering the positive implications of the injury can lead to better and quicker healing. Positives might include improvements in social networks (time available for friends), opportunities to improve the mental side of training (practicing goal setting, mindfulness, relaxation techniques, visualization, etc.), opportunities to become more resilient and for personal growth.

IMPORTANT PSYCHOLOGICAL COMPONENTS TO REHABILITATION:

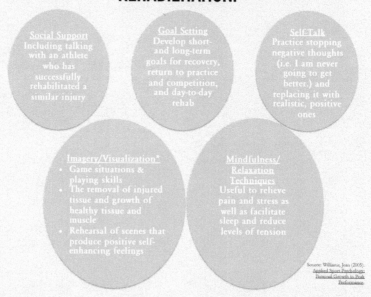

Social Support Including talking with an athlete who has successfully rehabilitated a similar injury

Goal Setting Develop short- and long-term goals for recovery, return to practice and competition, and day-to-day rehab

Self-Talk Practice stopping negative thoughts (i.e. I am never going to get better.) and replacing it with realistic, positive ones

Imagery/Visualization*
- Game situations & playing skills
- The removal of injured tissue and growth of healthy tissue and muscle
- Rehearsal of scenes that produce positive self-enhancing feelings

Mindfulness/ Relaxation Techniques Useful to relieve pain and stress as well as facilitate sleep and reduce levels of tension

Source: Williams, Jean (2005). Applied Sport Psychology: Personal Growth to Peak Performance

*The use of healing imagery/visualization has been shown in studies to characterize faster healing patients. Ask the doctor to explain and use pictures to show the exact healing process that needs to take place internally and you can start visualizing increased blood flow to the area, decreased swelling, stretching necessary for range of motion, etc.

APPENDIX B:
EXTRA WEEKLY CALENDARS

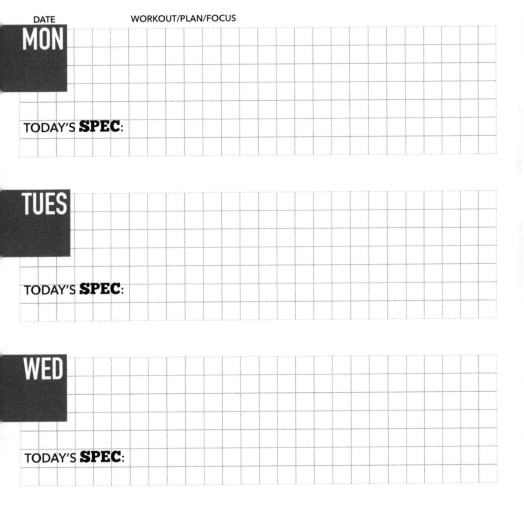

DATE	WORKOUT/PLAN/FOCUS
MON	

TODAY'S **SPEC**:

TUES

TODAY'S **SPEC**:

WED

TODAY'S **SPEC**:

WORKOUT/PLAN/FOCUS

DATE

THU

TODAY'S **SPEC**:

FRI

TODAY'S **SPEC**:

SAT

TODAY'S **SPEC**:

SUN

TODAY'S **SPEC**:

5 GRATITUDES FROM THE WEEK:

THIS WEEK'S INTENTION IN ONE WORD:

....

THE NUMBER OF BOTTLES OF WATER I PLAN TO HAVE EACH DAY THIS WEEK:

....

DATE   WORKOUT/PLAN/FOCUS

MON

TODAY'S **SPEC**:

TUES

TODAY'S **SPEC**:

WED

TODAY'S **SPEC**:

WORKOUT/PLAN/FOCUS

DATE

THU

TODAYS **SPEC**:

FRI

TODAY'S **SPEC**:

SAT

TODAY'S **SPEC**:

SUN

TODAY'S **SPEC**:

5 GRATITUDES FROM THE WEEK:

274

....

HOURS OF SLEEP I PLAN TO GET EACH NIGHT THIS WEEK:

....

....

DATE   WORKOUT/PLAN/FOCUS

MON

TODAY'S **SPEC**:

TUES

TODAY'S **SPEC**:

WED

TODAY'S **SPEC**:

WORKOUT/PLAN/FOCUS

DATE

THU

TODAY'S **SPEC**:

FRI

TODAY'S **SPEC**:

SAT

TODAY'S **SPEC**:

SUN

TODAY'S **SPEC**:

5 GRATITUDES FROM THE WEEK:

33 HABITS FOR FUELING PERFORMANCE (& FLOURISHING!)

1. BE KIND.
2. SURROUND YOURSELF WITH PEOPLE WHO LIFT YOU UP.
3. LIFT OTHERS UP.
4. PRACTICE SELF-COMPASSION.
5. FIND FLOW.
6. BRING MINDFULNESS INTO YOUR EVERY DAY.
7. MEDITATE.
8. GET OUTSIDE.
9. DREAM BIG.
10. CHOOSE ALTERNATIVES TO GOSSIP.
11. EXPRESS GRATITUDE.
12. VIEW STRESS AS A CHALLENGE, NOT A THREAT.
13. LET GO OF JUDGMENTS.
14. BELIEVE.
15. PRACTICE PURPOSEFULLY.
16. BE RECEPTIVE TO FEEDBACK (FOCUS—FEEDBACK—FIX IT).
17. SAY GOODBYE TO EXCUSES.
18. VIEW MISTAKES/FAILURES AS OPPORTUNITIES TO GROW.
19. EAT WELL.
20. DRINK WATER.
21. NOTICE AND SAVOR THE GOOD.
22. FOCUS ON THE PROCESS, NOT THE OUTCOME.
23. KEEP A HEALTHY SLEEP ROUTINE.
24. REFLECT (DAILY) ON GOOD THINGS.
25. FOCUS ON THE THINGS WITHIN YOUR CONTROL. LET GO OF WHAT YOU CAN'T.
26. BE COMFORTABLE BEING UNCOMFORTABLE.
27. CHOOSE OPTIMISM.
28. STICK TO YOUR VALUES.
29. CHOOSE TO BELIEVE HELPFUL THOUGHTS, NOT UNHELPFUL THOUGHTS.
30. BRING YOUR STRENGTHS FORWARD EVERY DAY.
31. PRACTICE VISUALIZATION.
32. STAND TALL AND THINK CONFIDENTLY.
33. CHOOSE TO BE UNSTOPPABLE OVER PERFECT.

UNSTOPPABLE.

UNSTOPPABLE /ADJ/:
THRIVING BY LEANING INTO
CHALLENGES AND/OR SETBACKS
WITH RELENTLESS EFFORT AND
CHARACTER